SALTWATER FISHING

Robert Anderson

A Great Outdoors Book

Great Outdoors Publishing Co.
St. Petersburg, Florida

Dedication

To my wife Dorothy, my daughter Robin,
and my sons Craig, Bruce, and Rickey.
All have enjoyed the sport of fishing
with an appreciative husband and father.

Table of Contents

About the Author

Robert Anderson was a man of varied interests, most of them related in one way or another to the great outdoors. He long had a consuming interest in, and knowledge of, snakes. He was also a devoted birdwatcher. A biologist by education and a motion picture cameraman by trade, he was a Florida outdoorsman by lifestyle. Fishing Florida waters has been high on his list of outdoor activities throughout the thirty years he lived here.

He filmed documentaries for all the major TV networks, served as a director of photography on the *Gentle Ben* and the *Flipper* series and authored a number of books, most on wildlife and environment. His book *Wilderness Florida* was published by VP Publications.

Acknowledgments

The author wishes to express his thanks to the National Marine Fisheries Service, an agency of NOAA (the National Oceanic and Atmospheric Administration), an agency of the United States Department of Commerce, and to IGFA (International Game Fish Association) and all of their most cooperative staff members for generously sharing technical advice and information on specific subjects related to their occupation.

INTRODUCTION

It is the purpose of this book to give in a convenient form a review of my knowledge concerning fishing in saltwater, along the coastlines, offshore, open water, and estuaries, and to make the final result of other specialists in the field accessible to those who enjoy and appreciate fishing and the fishes that abound in a saltwater wilderness.

Fishing is a general term, while angling is a particular kind of fishing. The word angling is supposed to have been derived from the bend of a hook, forming an angle; but the origin and antiquity of the term is comparatively unimportant now. It is sufficient to know that the art of angling "requires as much enthusiasm as poetry, as much patience as mathematics, and as much caution as housebreaking."

In order to pursue any branch of fishing with success, a knowledge of senses, habits and habitats of the fishes to be pursued should be carefully studied, regardless of the fishing method to be employed. So also should their food. They have their time to eat and their choice of food. It is commonly conceived that fishing is not as good as usual during easterly winds, but this is true only when winds cause coastal tides to rise so high that fish change their feeding grounds.

When is the best time to fish? In answer, I would like to quote an old saying for the diehard: "When the wind is in the east—fish bite the least, when in the west—fishing is at its best, when in the north—fishermen go forth, when in the south—the bait floats in the fish's mouth. The best time to fish is when you have the time."

1

Humankind has always held a special fascination for fish. Perhaps it is because fish belong to a world that is totally unlike ours. Possibly it is because there are so many kinds of fishes that there seem to be endless variations on an ever-changing theme. Perhaps it is because the fish, with its streamlined body, flashing silvery sides, and brilliant colors, seems so at home and so in harmony with our universe that we are moved to wonder and perhaps even feel a trace of envy.

Somehow, we equate fishing with peace and relaxation in a way that goes beyond the mere anticipation of a pleasant and nutritious meal. Even those who fish for a living seem to reflect an inner serenity, as if they absorbed some of the tranquility that fish seem to have. This is often reflected in the language of the fisherman, who never uses the word kill to describe their successes.

SALTWATER FISHING AS A SPORT

Back in the 1800s, saltwater fishing with "fancy" tackle (rod and reel) was mostly a rich person's sport. Wealthy sportsmen could afford to belong to exclusive fishing clubs where initiation fees ran up to $1,000. They could also afford to take days off, travel long distances, and buy the best saltwater fishing tackle—usually custom made. The average working person had to use an ordinary handline when fishing in the surf, from piers or boats.

But fishing with handlines wasn't very efficient or productive. One could not cast too far via the "heave and haul" method, and could not work artificial lures very well. And handline fishing didn't provide much fun or sport in fighting a fish.

The picture started to change right after World War I. Booming industries, higher wages, more leisure time and the automobile enabled people to travel to distant areas to go saltwater fishing. And fishing tackle manufacturers started to turn out better rods and reels at prices almost everyone could afford.

Today we have a wide variety of rods, reels, lures, and accessories for sale at our local bait and tackle shops, sporting goods stores, department stores, and other outlets. Or you can send for the catalogs advertised in many outdoor magazines.

Unlike hunters, who must think like their game to have a successful day's hunt, one can never think like a fish. Only after years of study can a careful observer learn his quarry's habits and anticipate a fish's movements and responses—but no mere human can know the sensations of vibrations striking a "lateral line." (See page 4.)

Until the middle of this century most people took it for granted that fish, as well as other living resources of the sea, were limitless.

3

Hadn't commercial fishermen been harvesting tuna in huge fish traps since the earliest days of the Christian era? Hadn't northern European seafarers been taking cod from the Grand Banks since before Columbus sighted San Salvador? But as the fish-catching ability of maritime nations grew at an explosive rate following World War II, it became apparent that many species of fish were in danger of following certain land-dwelling mammals and bird species into virtual extinction. Inland, in the narrow confines of freshwater rivers and lakes, it is easy to observe the effects of overfishing, pollution, and the destruction of habitat on vulnerable species. However, much is being done to rectify this problem by our local game and freshwater fish commissions, by federal agencies, by environmental organizations, and by members of our many fine fishing clubs. In confined, freshwater areas it is fairly easy to control size and bag limits with state laws. But to accomplish this in the open ocean is more difficult.

Working against conservation of species and habitat, including endangered marine fishes of the oceans, is the fact that on the high seas, beyond territorial limits, fish belong to everybody. Therefore, the cooperation of all nations is required to regulate overfishing and prevent misuse of the marine environment. Today, many countries are learning—and finally agreeing on—what constitutes conservation of marine species. Much has been done by our National Marine Fisheries Service, National Oceanic and Atmospheric Administration, to prevent the overfishing of mackerel, redfish, red snapper, snook, etc.

Through its "lateral line" a fish can determine directions in currents of water, detect the presence of nearby objects through variations in water pressure, and sense vibrations. This ability is useful to a fish in navigating at night or in murky waters, in keeping schooling fish together, in locating food, and in escaping predators. Lateral lines are distinctly shaped and of various lengths and are important sensory organs. All fish have a lateral line or two. (See illustration on the bottom of page 58.)

SALT- vs. FRESHWATER FISHING

Usually when an angler who is experienced in the ways of freshwater and its inhabitants makes his or her first contact with saltwater, he or she goes about it timidly, for even the water itself doesn't seem to look or act the same as it does inland. In addition, with such awesome expanses to look upon, the proposition of fishing becomes confusing. Where should he put down his or her line? Where are the fish going to be?

The fact is, saltwater *is* different in the way it "acts." But at the same time, many of the complex influences which bear upon the catching of fish in freshwater also apply in the ocean. For example, if water temperature is either too high or too low, fish become listless, no matter what kind of water they inhabit. Wind that muddies or cools the water will also inhibit fish. A falling barometer generally causes fish to lie close to the bottom and bite poorly, while a rising barometer will usually accentuate activity again; low or high oxygen content makes fish listless or active, respectively.

These influences and others act together, often in complex ways, to make fishing the wonderfully exciting game that it is. But another influence is stronger than all of these, in both fresh- and saltwater, but especially so in the latter. This is the tidal pull of the moon. Tidal influence is just as strong inland, but usually the bodies of water are too small to be appreciably affected, although the tidal pull undoubtedly influences the activity of fish. In saltwater, we can actually see the effect of the tides, and they govern directly much of the activity of all marine life, not alone by the mysterious moon pull, but far more by the action of currents and by lowering and raising the water levels several times each full day.

Therefore, to be a successful saltwater angler, one must understand this great influence. It is as important as the tackle one chooses. It is an interesting subject in itself, and related to angling, it will actually govern the size of the catch, almost without fail. In other words, the salty angler must plan his or her fishing in relation to the tides.

Tide terminology is as follows:
- incoming tide: toward shore
- high tide: crest of incoming tide
- outgoing tide: away from shore
- low tide: minimum low water level of outgoing tide

The varying water levels caused by tides radically change feeding conditions for fish, closing off or opening up new feeding grounds, covering and uncovering food, forcing forage fish to move, changing shallow water and beach contours. There are two low tides and two high tides on most days, roughly six hours apart.

Tides are caused by the pull of both sun and moon, but the moon's pull is stronger. A "moon day" (also known as a lunar or tidal day) is almost an hour longer than a sun (or solar) day. Therefore, each day every tide is a little later, and some days do not have four tides.

Most newspapers in coastal towns and cities print daily tide tables, giving the times and levels of each tide. The wise angler will follow them.

Tides cause currents. "Flood tide" means a shoreward current; an "ebb tide" is an offshore current. A "slack tide" means a maximum high or low, therefore no current. "Tide rips" are caused where opposing currents, brought about by quick depth changes or shore contours, oppose each other.

As a rule, fish feed most avidly on an incoming tide, then retire to deeper water on an outgoing tide. From an hour before high tide until an hour after is generally the peak of the feeding period. Currents and tide rips stir up food along shoals, bars, inlets, and passes, and are therefore hot spots for shore or near-shore anglers. Also, the half-hour to hour immediately following a slack tide, either low or high, usually sets the fish feeding, for the new water movement, whether inshore or offshore, stirs up food and causes small forage fish to move. Knowing these facts, an angler will have won the first battle in filling his or her live box or stringer, as well as assuring himself of hair-raising, unequalled sport. After learning all about the tides in relation to fishing saltwater, the angler must also learn the different kinds of fish he or she may catch, as well as their dominating influences.

ST. PETERSBURG TIMES

tides for Sunday, November 27

	High	Low	High	Low
St. Petersburg	2:28a	11:11a	....	....
Anna Maria	12:21a	8:40a		
Apalachicola	4:28a	1:55p	....	....
Bayport	1:56a	9:56a	4:14p	9:12p
Boca Grande	1:16a	9:15a		
Bradenton	1:04a	10:16a	....	....
Carrabelle	3:03a	11:42a		....
Cedar Key	2:26a	10:08a	4:44p	9:24p
Clearwater	12:35a	8:31a	2:53p	7:47p
St. Petersburg Beach Cswy	1:10a	10:27a	....	
Courtney Campbell Pkwy	4:03a	1:01p		....
Cortez	12:28a	9:46a	....	
Dunedin, St. Joseph Sound	12:33a	8:21a	2:51p	7:37p
Egmont Key	12:01a	8:47a		....
Englewood	1:31a	10:31a	....	
Gandy Bridge	3:35a	12:37p	....	....
Gulfport	12:56a	10:06a	....	....
Hillsborough Bay	2:35a	11:37a		
Indian Rocks	1:26a	9:13a	3:44p	8:29p
Johns Pass	12:14a	9:07a	....	
Little Manatee River	2:28a	11:11a		....
Madeira Beach Cswy	12:48a	9:53a	....	....
Naples	12:56a	8:34a	3:14p	7:50p
Pass A Grille	12:54a	9:41a	....	....
Pinellas Point	2:06a	10:42a	....	
Placida	1:01a	10:12a	....	....
Punta Gorda	3:34a	12:38p	....	
Punta Rassa	1:27a	9:52a		
St. Marks River Entrance	2:55a	10:38a	5:13p	9:54p
Safety Harbor	4:06a	1:06p	....	....
Sarasota	12:50a	10:13a	....	
Skyway Mullet Key Ent	12:06a	9:13a		
Steinhatchee River Ent	2:40a	10:35a	4:58p	9:51p
Suwanee River Entrance	2:29a	10:24a	4:47p	9:40p
Tarpon Springs, Anclote River	1:35a	9:25a	3:53p	8:41p
Venice	12:26a	9:33a		
Withlacoochee River Ent	2:30a	11:01a	4:48p	10:17p

Tomorrow's Key Tides

	High	Low	High	Low
St. Petersburg	3:22a	11:57a	....	....
St. Marks River Entrance	3:33a	11:21a	5:59p	10:43p

To compute tomorrow's tides, determine how much earlier or later than the key tide (St. Petersburg or St. Mark's) the tide is today at your point of interest. Tomorrow's tide will be the same amount of time earlier or later.

Gulf water temperature at Egmont Key 73 degrees.

7

SALTWATER TACKLE AND HOW TO USE IT

Methods of fishing in saltwater are no different than those used in freshwater fishing; only the tackle is different. The following tackle suggestions for use in your favorite way of fishing are outlined as a starting point. However, once you get the feel of things it is up to you, the angler, to select the most suitable tackle that will enable you to fish with comfort and yet be able to handle anything that challenges you.

BAIT CASTING TACKLE

Bait casting is usually described as the technique of casting an artificial bait or lure with a revolving-spool reel. Actually, this definition requires a bit of qualification. In reality, the bait casting rod and reel are specialized developments that are designed to cast artificial lures or baits to specific kinds of fish. From the early prototypes to the present machine-age equipment, many improvements have been made. The modern bait casting reel, for instance, is a descendent of those first perfected by Kentucky jewelers as early as 1810. Present-day reels have star drag and freespool devices, many are equipped with level-wind devices, and many have an anti-backlash device built into the reel. The great appeal of bait casting tackle is its versatility. A good quality outfit may be used for casting, trolling, live bait or bottom-fishing. Although your good freshwater bait casting tackle can be used in saltwater, it is definitely not advisable, because saltwater tackle should be rustproof and mineral-resistant to stand up to the corrosive nature of saltwater.

BAIT CASTING RODS

The length of your bait casting rod will depend on the kind of fishing you do, the weight of the lures or live bait cast, and whether you fish from a boat, from the shoreline, or wading a flat or shallow area. Many saltwater anglers who fish confined creeks and narrow canals that are lined with trees or brush use a short saltwater rod that allows easier casting among such shoreline obstacles; the same holds true for the angler casting similar areas from a boat. However, when casting from open shorelines or wading, longer rods are preferred, especially those with a limber action to cast lighter artificials and work them properly. Rods preferred by saltwater anglers have a longer butt section or handle.

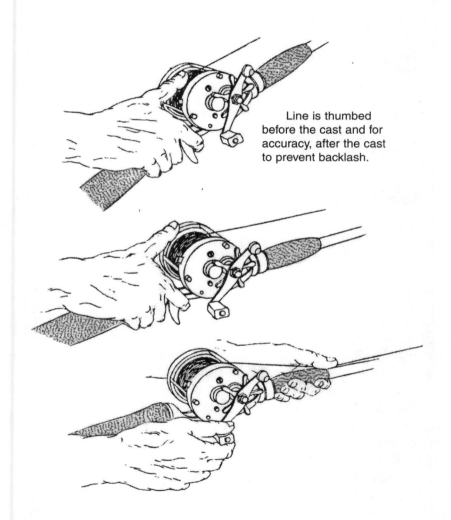

Line is thumbed before the cast and for accuracy, after the cast to prevent backlash.

BAIT CASTING REELS

Many saltwater anglers use a conventional free spool bait casting reel that is equipped with a level-wind mechanism and a lever or button that enables them to disengage gears, so

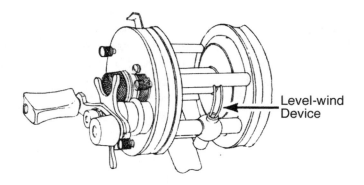

Level-wind
Device

that during the cast, the spool turns while the handle remains stationary. This helps to produce smoother, longer casts.

Many reels also are equipped with an anti-backlash device that can be adjusted to coincide with the weight of your artificial or natural bait.

When purchasing a reel for use in saltwater fishing, make sure that it is made of a non-corrosive metal.

SALTWATER BAIT CASTING ARTIFICIALS

Saltwater artificial baits are very similar to the freshwater kinds. However, plugs made for saltwater fishing offer resistance to saltwater corrosion. There are spoons of various kinds, up to $1\frac{1}{2}$ or 2 ounces, that are used for catching many different species of fish. The lighter spoons are more popular for trolling, but for casting the heavier ones are better. The action of spoons is changed by the speed used in retrieving them.

There are jigs made of bucktail, feathers, or nylon skirts; all are proven fish getters and can be successfully used to catch striped bass, weakfish (seatrout), tarpon, snook, Spanish and king mackerel, as well as many other species. Jigs weighing $\frac{1}{2}$ ounce upwards to 2 ounces are ideal for bait casting. Plugs of the popping kind, and swimming and crippled minnow types, are very effective in saltwater. They are used to catch fish species that prey on smaller fish, which they chase on the surface.

There are also many underwater artificials that resemble minnows. They come in silver and a wide variety of combinations of colors, some with different kinds of metal lips that create action, even deep diving, and then there are some that are straight and have to be worked into desired actions with the fishing rod tip.

And last but not least, the ever-popular plastic worms and eels are also used to catch saltwater fish, as are plastic jigs of many shapes.

HOW TO FIND BAIT CASTING GROUNDS

For the saltwater casting angler, the water's edge or a boat just offshore are ideal areas for using conventional bait casting or spin casting tackle with lightweight qualities. Bays, sounds, estuaries, and brackish-water rivers are ideal for this kind of fishing. Other areas that are good and easy to reach are the tidal creeks that wind in, through, and out of the saltwater marshlands. Here the angler fishes close to any undercut bank or deep hole, especially during the early mornings and at dusk during the incoming tide.

Another good area to fish is where a river empties into the ocean. Gamefish of many kinds usually wait for an incoming tide to bring their meals of shrimp, crabs and baitfish.

Bridges spanning inlets and channels are also good, as well as small, but deep creeks. In these places one can fish from the structure or from the shoreline or use a boat close enough to enable you to cast close to the banks.

Just remember that anywhere you choose to fish, always fish during and one hour after an incoming tide. The reason is that many of the areas just described are usually uncovered during the low tide period and fish will move in to feed during the incoming tide.

11

SURF CASTING

Surf casting is similar to freshwater bait or plug casting, except that it uses much heavier tackle, and both hands are used for making the cast. A long rod butt makes this possible. The cast usually is begun with the angler standing either close to the water's edge or ankle-deep in the surf. Like freshwater bait casting, the overhead cast is the most popular and the most often used.

SURF FISHING RODS

In choosing a surf rod, it is important to know where you will be fishing most of the time. Will it be from a sandy beach, a rocky shore, a jetty or some other location? Most beginners choose a spinning surf rod because it is easier to use and to cast with than the conventional types. Spinning surf rods can be broken down into three classes: light, medium and heavy. The light spinning surf rod will run from $7\frac{1}{2}$ to 9 feet in length. It is used with the smaller spinning reels, and 10-, 12-, or 15-pound test lines to cast lures up to two ounces. The medium-weight rod runs from 8 to 10 feet in length. It is used with larger spinning reels filled with 15- or 20-pound test line to cast lures up to 3 ounces. This rod is best for "all-around" fishing from the beach, rocky shores or jetties. The heavy spinning surf rod runs 10 to 14 feet and is used with a heavy-duty spinning reel loaded with 20- to 30-pound test lines; it will cast lures up to 4 or 5 ounces. This rod is good for big fish, long casts, and for bait fishing with heavy sinkers.

Surf rods come in one piece or in two sections. The longer one-piece rods must be transported outside the car. Two-piece rods break down so that they may be carried more easily.

REELS

Conventional surf reels have a revolving spool, free-spool lever, and star-drag; for best results they must be thumbed during the cast. They are still used by some surf anglers for big fish and bait fishing, but surf spinning reels are more popular today and are definitely best for the beginner. The open-faced surf spinning reels come in various sizes and

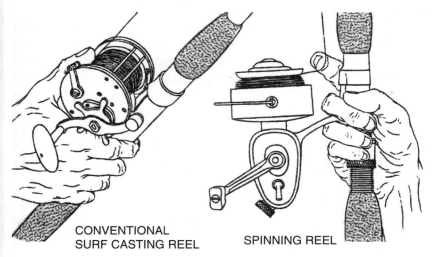

CONVENTIONAL
SURF CASTING REEL   SPINNING REEL

weights and hold anywhere from 200 to 400 yards of line, depending on the pound test the angler prefers. Small-sized surf reels are used with light surf spinning rods; larger reels with medium rods, and the biggest reels with the heaviest surf rods. An ideal combination for all surf casting is a medium/heavy action rod, 9 feet in length that will cast a 1.4-ounce lure or live bait with ease; reel should be a spinning reel with a gear ratio of 4.3:1. Line should be monofilament, with a test of 15 or 20 pounds. Lures upwards to 3 ounces may be used with this rig.

LINES

Monofilament lines testing 20 to 45 pounds can be used on a conventional reel. For surf spinning reels, monofilament lines testing from 10 to 30 pounds are used, with lighter lines best for light tackle, small fish, and light lures. For big fish, heavy lures, and when fishing in rocky areas or in heavy surf and strong currents, a 20- or even 40-pound test line can be used.

SURF RIGS

For bait fishing in the surf, two rigs are popular. One is the standard rig, where the hook on the leader is tied to a three-way swivel a few inches above the sinker. The other is the "fish-finder rig," where a ring and snap moves up and down the line; the snap holds the sinker and the line is threaded through the ring (as illustrated). A barrel swivel acts as a stop for the sinker and the leader and hook are tied to the swivel. Pyramid sinkers weighing from 3 to 5 ounces, depending on the weight of the rod, are usually used with a medium to heavy action surf rod when fishing sandy beaches. In rocky areas you can use bank or round sinkers, available in many weights.

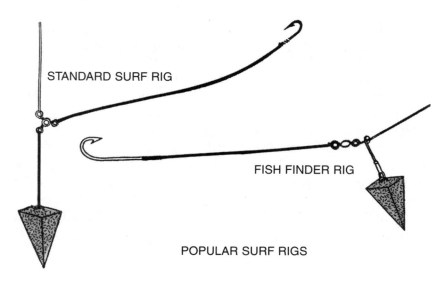

STANDARD SURF RIG

FISH FINDER RIG

POPULAR SURF RIGS

SURF "SHOCK LEADER" TO LINE KNOT

1. When leader is five times or more the pound/test of line, double ends of both leader and line back about 6 inches. Slip loop of line through loop of leader far enough to permit tying Uni-Knot around both strands of leader.

2. With doubled line, tie Uni-Knot around the two strands of leader, using only four turns.

3. Put finger through loop of line and grasp both tag end and standing line to pull knot snug around loop of leader.

4. With one hand, pull standing leader (not both strands). With other hand, pull both strands of line (see arrows). pull slowly until knot slides to end of leader loop and all slippage is, gone.

Surgeon's End Loop

Use this knot to tie a loop in the end of a line for attaching leaders or other terminal tackle quickly.

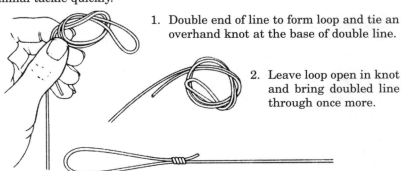

1. Double end of line to form loop and tie an overhand knot at the base of double line.

2. Leave loop open in knot and bring doubled line through once more.

3. Hold standing line and tag end and pull loop to tighten knot. Size of loop can be determined by pulling loose knot to desired point and holding it while knot it tightened. Clip tag end.

MAKING THE SURF CAST

Surf casting is similar to bait casting, except that with such heavy tackle both hands must be used to make the cast. The long rod handle, or butt, makes this possible. The cast is begun with the angler standing either close to the water's edge or perhaps ankle-deep in the surf. The angler faces parallel to the shoreline, with rod tip pointing shoreward, the rod held about mid-chest high and at almost right angles to his or her body, the tip dipping slightly. The right hand grips the butt near the reel (which is placed near the top of the butt), thumb upon the reel spool. The left hand grips the far end of the rod butt. By keeping the hands widely spaced, greater power of swing, and therefore greater distance of cast, is possible. The sinker and bait, or casting lure, is allowed to lie on the sand with a couple of feet of line between it and rod tip, until cast is made.

Making the cast requires nothing but a powerful up-and-over swing, thumb holding the reel spool firmly until the rod has reached almost a vertical position. The reel is then released, and the bait and sinker travel high and swiftly out over the waves. Meanwhile, the angler follows through with the rod, swinging the right leg around so that, as the bait hits the water, he or she is facing the spot where it has landed, and the angler's back is to the shore. The surf casting method just described is for a free-spooling conventional reel. For spin-casting in the surf, hold the rod with the right hand at the reel seat with the thumb on top and the other fingers below (as illustrated). Two fingers can be placed in front of the leg or support of the reel and two behind. Left hand holds the rod butt. With the bailer pulled down and back into the lock position, with your left hand turn the reel handle until the

16

line roller is on top; then pick up the line with the index finger of the right hand. Back off the reel handle so that the line is freed from the roller, after which the left hand pushes the wire bail down until it locks in the casting position. Bring the rod up to shoulder height with reel facing up. Next, with a

When using a conventional reel, thumb must hold line spool at the beginning of the cast.

Bailer is in locked position and the angler is holding the line with forefinger of the reel hand (left).

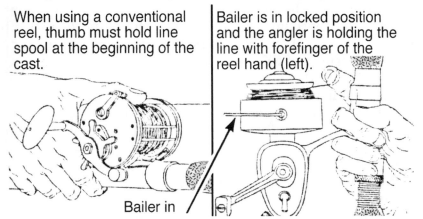

Bailer in

quick motion, bring the rod tip up over your head. The tip will bend in an arc and then start to propel the bait forward, at which time you should release the line from your finger and bring the rod down, with the tip pointing toward the target. When the bait reaches the target, bring your finger down to the lip of the spool to stop your cast. Timing is the most important factor in casting, along with the "feel" of the weight of the bait or sinker. Release the bailer, crank in excess slack, and you are ready to experience one of the greatest methods of saltwater fishing.

A surf belt—a leather belt with a heavy leather cup to receive the butt of the rod—is a must for the surf angler, especially should one be angling for large stripers or a shark. Another must is a "spike," or rod holder, for still-fishing with live bait in the surf—the most popular, easiest and most effective method in general. There are several types of rod holders. The spike is a steel rod or flattened steel band, usually about three feet in length, sharpened on one end so it can be shoved deep down into the sand. On the other end there is an aperture—an iron ring or some other device into which the rod butt may be slipped and solidly held. Thus, after the cast, the rod may be slipped into the spiked top. This eases the work for the angler and serves to hold the rod up high, which keeps the line out of the wash of the breakers. By watching the rod tip, the angler can tell the instant a strike is made. The angler then simply slips the rod out of the holder, sets the hook and drops the rod butt into the belt cup to fight the fish. Surf anglers can make their own rod holder from a flat steel band and a short length of PVC pipe. There are two kinds, either of which will serve the purpose (see illustration). A suggestion to the angler: when placing the rod holder into the sand, do not place it in an extreme vertical position, but instead slant it backwards a bit (see illustration). I have stood by helplessly as a fish pulled the rod out to sea because the pole holder was slanted seaward and the drag was tightly set on the reel. Another hint is never to set the drag too tight; it is best to set it *after* the fish hits and you pull the rod from the holder and have it tightly in your hands. Of course, if you feel that you have everything under control for a big hit, preset your drag and be ready.

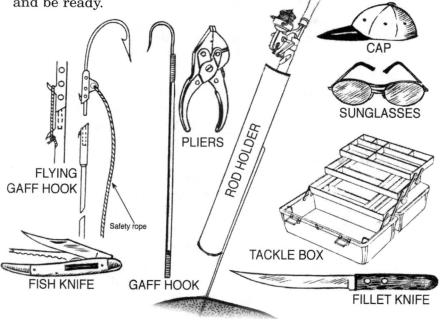

CAP

SUNGLASSES

FLYING GAFF HOOK

Safety rope

PLIERS

ROD HOLDER

TACKLE BOX

FISH KNIFE

GAFF HOOK

FILLET KNIFE

SURF FISHING LURES AND BAITS

Heavy, spoon-type lures are good, as are the assorted metal "squids." These are usually made of stainless steel or other metals which are chrome or nickel-plated. Your old casting plugs—the large ones that were used in northern freshwaters, are also ideal. These include surface and diving types including poppers, swimmers, and crippled baitfish, lures that move on the surface and create a commotion. These plugs are ideal for all kinds of fish that feed in the surf: bluefish, redfish, striped bass, etc. When stripers are running and feeding in the shoreline, underwater plugs that dive and travel just below the surface or a few feet below are good, but few artificials can surpass your largest largemouth bass bait, the plastic worm or eel. They must, however, be not less than ten inches in length and have an action head that provides casting weight and gives the lure an eely, lifelike movement. Eels should be reeled at slow speeds for best results, especially at night. when they are particularly effective. When in the shoreline and not wearing waders, it is best to wear sneakers to protect your feet from getting cuts from broken shell debris, as well as for protection against stingrays, which have the habit of burying themselves in the sand. A stab or laceration from a stingray's tail-spine can be very painful and should be treated immediately with an antiseptic. Should the spine break off in the foot, seek medical help at once.

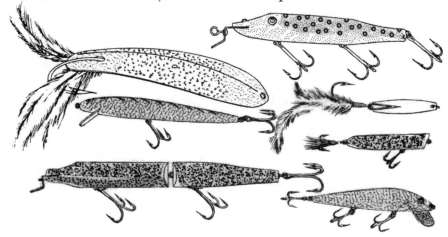

SURF CASTING

What bait should you use in the surf? That depends on what you are expecting to catch, and the method used to get it beyond the breakers. Casting will usually limit you to the use of a medium-sized mullet, chunk bait or other small baits like shrimp, squid, crab or a large lure.

The proper setting of a hook when fishing in the surf should be done with your rod held parallel to the ground or water, and then with a sharp twist at the waist. This action places your entire body weight, rather than just the strength of your wrist and arms, behind the rod tip. Remember, a sharp hook is always a must.

Keep gloves available for grabbing your line or leader to beach a large fish. An even better method is to use a gaff hook, and for fish weighing more than 25 pounds, a flying-gaff should be used.

Landing a large fish in heavy surf isn't easy, but it can be made more so by letting the incoming surf work for you. *Never* attempt to drag a large fish through outgoing breakers. Such an action can snap the line, straighten the hook or tear the fish off the hook. Instead, pump and crank your fish in on each crest of an incoming breaker, but only allow it to slide back on a taut line, with the undertow. When your timing is right you will be able to keep the fish coming on a wave that will eventually beach your fish, high and dry. It is at this time that you either grab the line or leader or drive your gaff home and beach your catch.

CAUTION should be heeded when fishing in the surf!

1. When wading in heavy surf, keep your eyes on the incoming breakers; never turn your back to them.
2. Never wade out too far if the breakers are strong, or if a great pull of the undertow is obvious.
3. Never wear hip boots—if anything, wear chest-high waders. If the surf is warm, long pants or shorts can be worn, but always wear boat shoes, sneakers, or beach shoes to protect your feet from sharp rocks and broken seashells, and from the spines of a resting stingray or sea urchin.
4. Never tie a stringer of fish to your waist while deep in the surf. This can attract sharks and barracudas. Tie your stringer to a long pole stuck deep into the sand, or to a special rig close to the beach in about one to two feet of water.

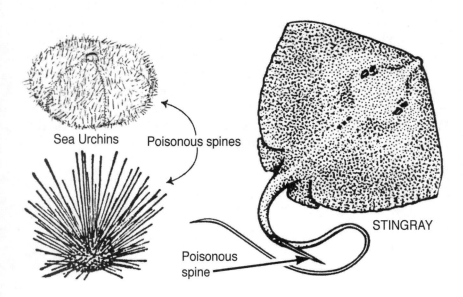

Sea Urchins   Poisonous spines

Poisonous spine

STINGRAY

WHERE TO FISH IN THE SURF

Finding fish or fishing areas along the surf may be rather difficult for the novice angler. It is best to try to locate areas along the beach where other anglers are fishing. If fish are being caught you can join them, but don't get so close that you interfere with their fishing. Many old-timers will ignore you unless you are loud and rowdy and moving all over the beach. On the other hand, many local tackle shops will offer advice as to a good place to surf cast. If you are entirely on your own, look for evidence that suggests a productive area, such as the color of the water that usually indicates its depth. Dark blue or dark green usually indicate deep waters, sloughs or channels. Should the water be a light green or brown with stirred up sand, or white with strong wave action, this may prove to be a sand bar or shallow area. When such areas are covered with water, they often have surf fish that are in season. Strong wave action usually washes out crabs and sand fleas into a slough, the deep area between a sand bar and the beach, and surf fish often occupy the inside of the bar to feed on these tasty crustaceans. Many bars have cuts and breaks that provide good fishing. Some beaches have rock jetties spaced at regular intervals. These often provide excellent fishing, especially when bait and rig are laid very close to the rocks or in the deep holes formed by a stack of rocks.

SALTWATER TROLLING

Trolling is another popular method for catching fish. Trolling is comparable to drift fishing in that both methods allow the angler to cover a lot of ground. Some anglers refer to trolling as the most popular and important saltwater method. Those anglers fortunate enough to own a seaworthy boat, or able to afford to charter or rent one, will be challenged by a great variety of fish species from all depths of the sea. Should the first time out be successful, the angler is spoiled for life, and will resent having to fish by any other method. I have been very successful in trolling the seas, but I have also been very successful in surf casting. Given the choice, I say "give me a surf when the stripers are running and I will leave trolling to the other anglers—that is, unless the dolphins, king mackerel, and billfishes are on a feeding binge."

Trolling in the bays and just offshore with a small boat is often very rewarding. Just be sure that your craft has all the safety equipment required by the Coast Guard.

Many saltwater fish travel in large schools and roam widely. By trolling, one of these huge schools can usually be located. Or, for those large saltwater prizes that are solitary travelers, trolling is the equivalent of big game hunting. It is like stalking big gamefish.

Trolling near the surface is the most popular, for it is easiest and eliminates the use of exceedingly large sinkers, needed to get the bait or lure down to great depths. Nearly all salt-water gamefish which are commonly taken by trolling can be found at some time of day, or tide, near the surface.

Small boat trolling in bays, lagoons, channels, etc., differs in no way from freshwater trolling. The lure (or natural bait) is simply tossed overboard and allowed to run out some distance behind the boat. With artificials, it is common in salt-water, both in casting and trolling, to give the rod a long sweep, or jerk, every couple of seconds. In casting, this is done by jerking the rod tip, then reeling in the slack caused by such rod action, and continually repeating the process. The motion caused by the jerking of the rod tip is transferred to the lure, presenting lifelike action that is particularly attractive to most saltwater fish.

For trolling in open water for larger saltwater gamefish, there are several differences for regulation trolling.

Flat trolling is one method. It means you troll by the usual method, sitting at the stern of the boat, holding the rod, letting the line run straight back. This has many disadvantages. It means only one person at a time can successfully work a line in open water. It is back-breaking work, when you must hold heavy tackle against the pull of the long, heavy line and bait. It is difficult to fashion and hook up bait such as strips of fish or whole fish in such a way that flat trolling won't soon rip them from the hook or tear them to pieces.

Outrigger trolling has therefore been developed to over-come the difficulties of deep-sea flat trolling. This method is the one used on virtually all deep-sea charter boats. The out-rigger is a long pole, several of which are placed at various angles sticking out and upward from the sides and stern of

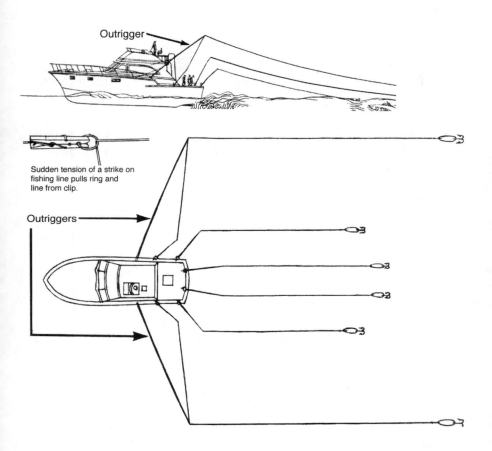

Outrigger

Sudden tension of a strike on
fishing line pulls ring and
line from clip.

Outriggers

the trolling boat. Regular tackle is set up, but the line from
each rod is held to the end of an outrigger by a clip and held
high in the air, and the bait, far behind, is made to skip entic-
ingly along the surface by adjusting the speed of the boat.
When a strike comes, the line is yanked from its outrigger
holder, the angler grabs the rod, sets the hook, and the fight
is on. Several trollers are able to fish simultaneously from the
same boat without getting fouled. There is less water pull on
the line, and less wear and tear on the angler and bait.

FOUR POPULAR SALTWATER
DEEP TROLLING METHODS

There are, at the present time, four popular trolling methods or systems being used by saltwater anglers. All work very well and are very productive. They are:

1. The so-called multiple-depth, multiple-lure system, which includes the use of a heavy fixed weight and any number of artificial and natural baits.
2. The expendable-weight drip-sinker system.
3. The fish-planer, or what is referred to as a paravane system
4. The downrigger system, fast becoming popular

Of the four methods, the first three are utilized without wire fishing lines; in a downrigger system, a wire fishing line may be used. However, all four systems may be trolled with the use of a motor-driven boat, and except for the downrigger method all call for the use of common, conventional tackle. Only the downrigger requires the use of elaborate tackle.

Depth of bait on all systems is controlled by the length of fishing line trailing the boat. The planer sometimes calls for more line and/or faster boat speed.

THE MULTIPLE-DEPTH SYSTEM: Here the fishing line must be at least a medium trolling line with a 30-, to 40-pound breaking test. All hardware line swivels, snaps, etc. should be made of brass. Brass swivels should be placed between sections separating the branch lines, usually separated at 9- to 18-foot intervals. Branch lines are made of main line material which should be between 10 to 30 feet in length (as illustrated). Tackle, such as rod reel and main line, must be heavy enough to control and support several pounds of rigged tackle, bait included—and of course one, two or more fighting fish.

This multiple-depth method is very effective in that it permits the angler to cover and explore considerable depths of water levels. Its origin is linked to commercial fishing, and because of this an angler should check with local authorities governing saltwater deep trolling before utilizing the rig; some areas outlaw its use.

Tackle: Use a 1- to 2-pound ball, dipsey or sand-fixed sinker. Brass snap-swivels may be used for attaching baited

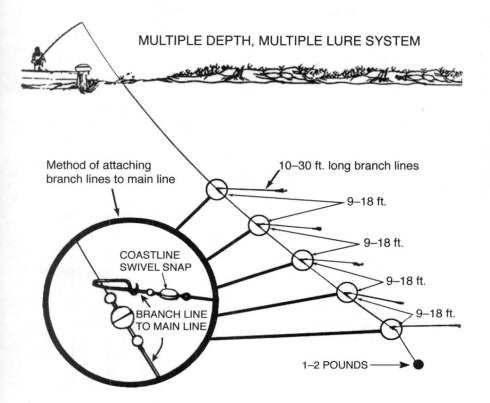

MULTIPLE DEPTH, MULTIPLE LURE SYSTEM

Method of attaching
branch lines to main line

10–30 ft. long branch lines

9–18 ft.

9–18 ft.

9–18 ft.

COASTLINE
SWIVEL SNAP

9–18 ft.

BRANCH LINE
TO MAIN LINE

1–2 POUNDS ⟶

hooks or lures, spoons, spinners, and wooden or plastic lures. When using lures, a lightweight surface plug should be secured to the uppermost branch-line, and to the bottom branch-line a diving lure should be attached. Spinners and spoons may be used on the remaining, in-between branches. Troll at a slow speed when using this rig. Last, but not least, if unfamiliar with the ocean's bottom, a release-sinker device may be utilized so that there is less chance of losing your entire rig should the sinker get hung up on a rock or underwater marine debris. (For an example, see the release sinker device that follows the planer rig).

THE EXPENDABLE-WEIGHT DEEP TROLLING RIG:
Like the planer rig, this system allows only one artificial or
natural bait to be used on a line. However, the big advantage
here is that when a fish is hooked the weight of the heavy
sinker is removed from the line, making fishing much more
enjoyable and causing less wear and tear on the angler and
tackle. Weight used is usually a ball sinker which has a wire
eye that can be conveniently attached to the sinker release
device. However, a heavy sand (pyramid) or dipsey sinker
(each with a wire eye) may be used.

THE EXPENDABLE-WEIGHT DROP SINKER SYSTEM

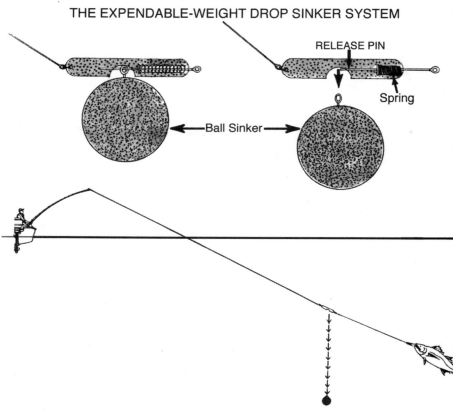

Sinker-release device: A sinker-release may be used in
almost all trolling rigs. A commercial sinker release may be
purchased, or one can make use of the self-rigged sinker

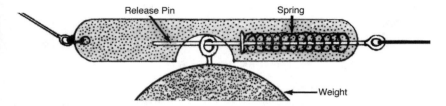

Release Pin

Spring

Weight

release illustrated on page 28. The commercial device is made of a metal or plastic cylinder with an eye on each end for connecting the mainline, and an internal spring and sliding pin designed to hold a ball sinker. The ball sinker is the most popular sinker used by the serious trolling angler. It has a wire eye molded into it that slips onto the release pin. When a strike occurs, the sudden added line tension pulls back the release pin and the sinker falls to the bottom and gives the angler a free line to play the fish and land it. In an emergency, many anglers use a large dipsey or a sand sinker, both of which have a wire eye for convenience.

THE PLANER RIG: This method of trolling involves a metal or plastic diving device that has a heavy, well-designed towing yoke (as illustrated) which is attached to the main line with a ball bearing snap swivel. The baited trail-line is connected to the other end of the planer with a coast-lock swivel snap. The two snaps should be of heavy, good quality brass.

THE METAL PLANER

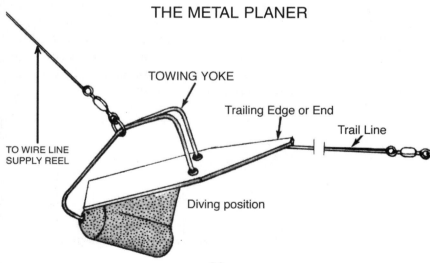

TOWING YOKE

Trailing Edge or End

Trail Line

TO WIRE LINE
SUPPLY REEL

Diving position

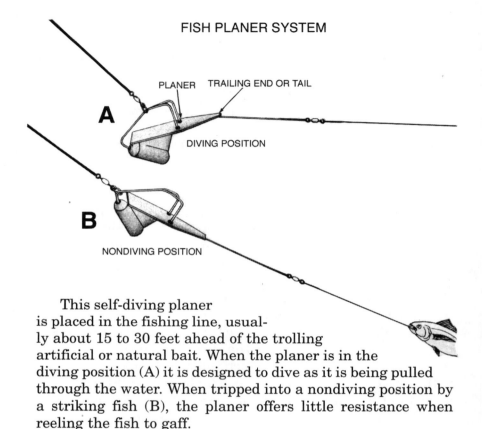

FISH PLANER SYSTEM

PLANER   TRAILING END OR TAIL

A

DIVING POSITION

B

NONDIVING POSITION

This self-diving planer
is placed in the fishing line, usually about 15 to 30 feet ahead of the trolling
artificial or natural bait. When the planer is in the
diving position (A) it is designed to dive as it is being pulled
through the water. When tripped into a nondiving position by
a striking fish (B), the planer offers little resistance when
reeling the fish to gaff.

Many anglers use a planer in a different way, by attaching
a line-release device such as the one used with a downrigger
(as illustrated below), to the trailing edge or tail of the planer. The depth of the planer depends on the speed of the boat
and the amount of the trailing line. Trolling should be done at
slow to moderate speeds when using a planer.

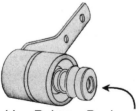

Line Release Device as used in a Downrigger

OPERATING THE PLASTIC ECONOMY PLANER

1. Attach your rod line to the DIP-PER DIVER trip line swivel.

2. Attach 3 to 7 feet of leader to tail line swivel.

3. Attach desired lure.

4. Set a starboard course for your Dipper Diver by turning the control tab to the right (Fig' 1). To direct the Big Dipper Diver to run port side turn the control tab to the left (Fig. 2). Send the diver downward by positioning the control tab below the weight and tail (Fig. 3),

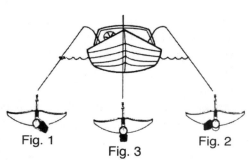

Fig. 1

Fig. 3

Fig. 2

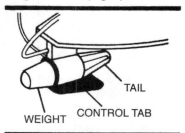

TAIL

WEIGHT CONTROL TAB

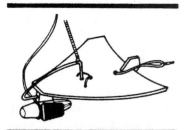

5. You should now be able to trip your Big Dipper by pulling your rod forward without jerking.

6. You may set and unset the Big Dipper in the water by moving the rod forward to unset it and then dropping the rod tip back to reset it.

7. Big Dipper Diver will unset itself if it strikes the bottom.

8. Sensitivity settings for the Big Dipper Diver are diagramed at right.

9. Trip and reset and repeat to allow flutter trolling length.

→

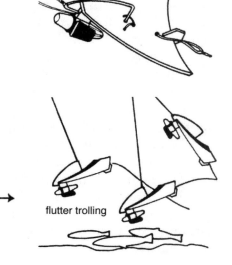

flutter trolling

DEEP-TROLLING WITH THE DOWNRIGGER

The downrigger is an underwater outrigger that carries a fishing rig to practically any depth you desire. When using a downrigger, trolling depth is controlled by a heavy weight of special design that is lowered over the side or stern of a boat, most often on the end of a stainless steel wire line. This wire line is stored on a special hand reel that usually has some sort of line measuring or revolution-counting device to display exactly how much line is out at any given time.

This method of fishing deep with light lines was first used in freshwater by anglers deep trolling for salmon. Today there is a ready market for saltwater non-corrosive units. Although the basic concept has never really changed, additional features—such as electric retrieval mechanisms and water temperature readouts at the depth being trolled. Additional uses for downriggers include holding a chum can or pot on the bottom during a strong current when fishing for grouper and snapper. Unlike a fish line, the wire holding the downrigger does not develop a belly, which makes it easy to wind up a heavily weighted chum-pot for a refill. So sophisticated are some of the new designs of downriggers that some are equipped with computerized additions—for instance, a control pad which allows the angler not only to enter, but to store and change depths; direct vertical movement of the downrigger weight during its retrieval; oscillation of the bait, artificial or natural, at different speeds and depths; and information about where the bait is. All saltwater versions are constructed of materials impervious to saltwater corrosion. Booms are usually of made of stainless steel, as are the components used with it. Bodies are usually made of Lexan polycarbonate. Most downriggers come equipped with 400 feet of stainless steel cable, reel, depth meter, and adjustable-angle rod hold, snap swivel and a positive deckplate locking wheel. Standard-length booms are usually about 18 inches; standard plus 42 and 66 inches are optional. Many can be upgraded from manual to electric to computerized. There is one late-model downrigger that is equipped with an interesting innovation that automatically provides a forward or upward darting motion to

DOWNRIGGER TROLLING SYSTEM

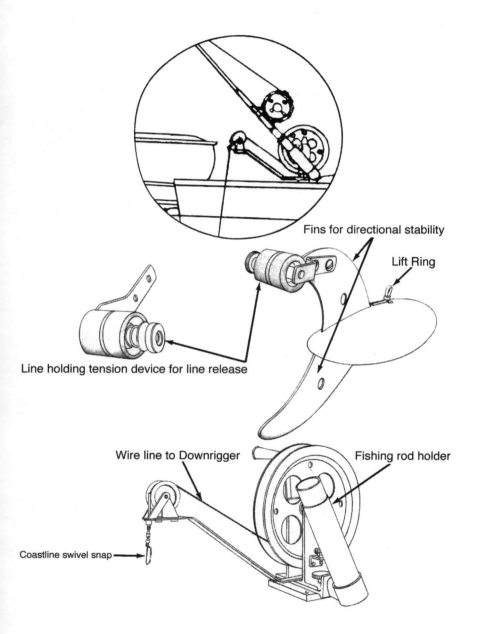

Fins for directional stability

Lift Ring

Line holding tension device for line release

Wire line to Downrigger

Fishing rod holder

Coastline swivel snap

the bait. This model consists of a compact, sealed container with a rod holder on the top.

The weight, of special design, is equipped with an outrigger type of line release. This release may be in the form of a springloaded jaw device or a twin-roller device as displayed in the illustration above. In the latter design, the line is placed between the rollers after the lure or natural bait is trailing the boat at about 20 to 30 feet. At this time both the downrigger weight and fishing line are lowered at the same time to the desired trolling depth, which will be recorded on your counting device on the hand reel. This depth may be as little as a few feet below the boat, or it may be at the location of a "thermocline" (see page 36) in much deeper water.

When a fish hits or strikes at the bait, the fishing line is pulled from between the jaws or rollers of the line release device and the angler plays the fish without a heavy annoying conventional sinker. It is at this time that a fishing partner hauls up the downrigger and drops back a baited rig, clips the line into the downrigger's line-release device, and lowers it to the desired depth, while the first fish is being hauled in and the fish below are on a feeding binge.

This all sounds very easy, but fishing with a downrigger calls for the angler to be constantly aware of the depth under the boat. Gaining this knowledge quickly and conveniently calls for the use of portable or permanent electronic sounding instrument. A sounder serves at least three primary purposes:

1. It indicates the water depth and the characteristics of the bottom.
2. It indicates fish under the boat.
3. It indicates rocks and other obstructions that must be avoided to prevent damage to the downrigger equipment.

The illustration on the following page displays a hooked fish on the downrigger and a second line being put into the water which will replace the rod in the holder of the downrigger while the hooked fish is being played and landed. Meanwhile, the second angler is watching the sounder and observes that the boat is moving over a rocky area. He will quickly reel in some of the downrigger line, lifting the weight above the rocks. The downrigger weight will actually be seen on the screen of the sounding device along with the rocky area.

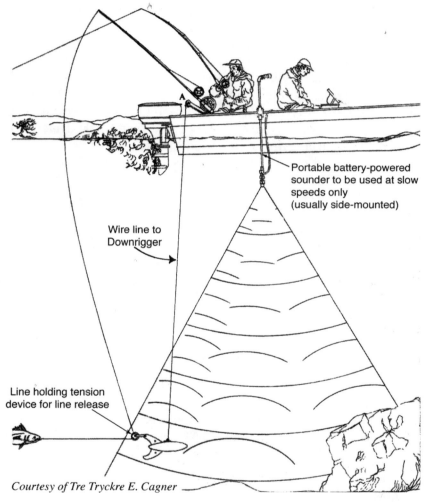

Portable battery-powered sounder to be used at slow speeds only (usually side-mounted)

Wire line to Downrigger

Line holding tension device for line release

Courtesy of Tre Tryckre E. Cagner

Downriggers are one of the best, most advanced methods for trolling. They alleviate the use of the old trolling sinkers (the Drail and the Keel) that caused a lot of wear and tear on the tackle as well as the angler (see illustration on page 46).

Downriggers are much more sophisticated than the early ones described above. They are now equipped with an electric motor drive to raise and lower the weights, and with extension rods so that as many as four downriggers can be used simultaneously, two astern and two over the sides from a single boat. All work very well in depths of more than 165 feet at trolling speeds of under four knots. A downrigger weight, usually made of cast iron, weighs between 11 and 15 pounds, and the wire connected to it usually tests at 75 to 80 pounds.

Thermocline layer: In general, the temperature in the ocean decreases rapidly from the surface downward. Typically there are three layers. There is a mixed, or isothermal, layer at the surface which may be 60 to 600 feet thick. Below the mixed layer is a thin zone called the thermocline in which there is a rapid drop in temperature. Below the thermocline, temperature decreases gradually.

SUGGESTED TROLLING SPEEDS
(For conventional tackle only;
does not include trolling with a planer or downrigger)

SPECIES	SPEED	SPECIES	SPEED
Albacore	4–7 mph	Striped Marlin	3–6 mph
Amberjack	3–5 mph	White Marlin	4–7 mph
Barracuda	2–4 mph	Sailfish, Atlantic	3–5 mph
Striped Bass	2–5 mph	Sailfish, Pacific	3–5 mph
Bluefish	3–4 mph	Weakfish, Spotted	2–3 mph
Bonefish	2–3 mph	Snook	2–3 mph
Cobia	3–5 mph	Swordfish	3–6 mph
Dolphin	4–8 mph	Tarpon	2–3 mph
Black Drum	3–4 mph	Tuna, Bluefin	3–7 mph
King Mackerel	3–6 mph	Tuna, Yellowfin	4–8 mph
Black Marlin	4–6 mph	Wahoo	7–8 mph
Blue Marlin (Atl.)	4–6 mph	Yellowtail, Southern	3–5 mph
Blue Marlin (Pac.)	5–8 mph		

SHARK	SPEED	SHARK	SPEED
Blue	3–5 mph	Hammerhead, Great	3–5 mph
Mako	3–6 mph	Thresher	3–5 mph
Porbeagle	3–6 mph	White	2–4 mph

Occasionally Tiger sharks are caught while deep trolling at speeds of 3 to 4 mph, which also happens to be an ideal average speed for all species that are usually caught by a trolling system.

WHERE TO TROLL OFFSHORE

Finding fish in a large body of water like the ocean is not easy, but it is possible. Before starting out, be sure that your craft is seaworthy to go where you want to fish. A word of advice before going out on what could wind up to be a wild goose chase: Be sure to get as much information as you can about the saltwater territory you intend to cover, either from local anglers or boaters, or by consulting local newspapers and magazines, and most especially from NOAA charts.

As suggested in the introduction of this book, for the first time out, try to hire a guide or charter a small boat. It is well worth the expense, as the big salty sea is not a playground. Your guide can suggest natural baits, lures, rigs and methods used to catch certain fish. Should you decide to go it alone, search for fish with binoculars; look for the dark spots in the water where there is a ruffled or rippled surface, slicks, splashes, or floating objects, especially seaweed patches, for under this cover usually swim the tenacious dolphins (the fish). Also look for birds hovering, for when they gather offshore it usually means that large gamefish are chasing bait fish to the surface. Frequently you may be able to see baitfish leaping clear of the water during their attempt to escape the jaws of the predators. All disturbances, even the slightest, should be investigated.

Another good bet is to watch for other fishing boats, especially those in a group and pulling in fish; try fishing in the general area. Sometimes a large fleet of private boats will be found trolling the same area, chumming and drifting, or even anchored in a particular area. Most offshore anglers use electronic aids that record depths and/or locate fish. If you have a marine radio, tune in because many skippers get on the air report to others how they are doing.

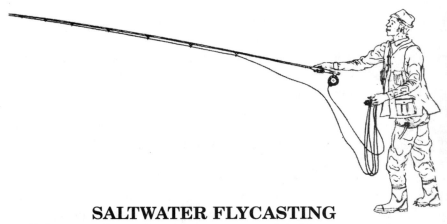

SALTWATER FLYCASTING

Saltwater flycasting is a sport practiced by many saltwater anglers. However, it is not a sport for the newly-baptized saltwater angler! But it is a fantastically exciting venture for the seasoned freshwater fly-fisherman. Although a regular freshwater fly rod of bass weight may be used it is best to buy a rod that is built for this type of fishing. There are many good saltwater fly rods made of fiberglass that are equipped with stainless steel guides and anodized aluminum reel seats which will not corrode in saltwater. In fact, some manufacturers have gone as far as designing saltwater rods that a detachable extension butt that can be added to the end of the rod to provide additional leverage for the angler when fighting a large fish.

It is not surprising to see some of the expert saltwater fly anglers challenging the likes of large tarpon, snook, and even some of the bill fishes.

As a general rule, surface flies are usually nowhere near as successful in saltwater as they are in freshwater. However, tarpon, striped bass, and a few other species have been known to take them at times. Most types of artificials are in the form of "popping bugs," like or very similar to the large ones used for largemouth bass. The standards that prove most successful for a great variety of saltwater fish are the streamer flies in yellows, red, whites, etc. Bucktails in the same colors, and metal spinners, are excellent as are a variety of spoons.

FLYCASTING REELS

In selecting a saltwater fly reel, one must take into consideration that most saltwater fish usually caught on fly tackle make longer runs than those caught in freshwater, except for salmon or steelheads. Therefore, the reel should have a large capacity and be loaded with plenty of backing line. But here again, manufacturers have designed special reels featuring non-corrosive parts, large line capacity, and a dependable drag. For most of the larger fly rod lures the line will give best results if it is of the "forward taper" (torpedo-head) type, of a size and weight, to match rod action and length. Many fly reels are made with a quick-release spool for easily changing from one kind of line to another. This allows the angler to build a very versatile line system, ready for everything. Floating lines are considered best for all-round fishing, but sinking lines can also be used when you want your lures to get down deep. The most popular sizes for saltwater are WF9F WF10F, and WF11F.

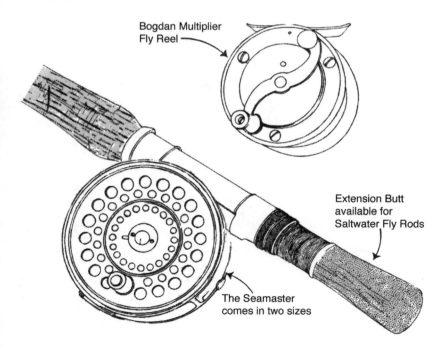

Bogdan Multiplier
Fly Reel

Extension Butt
available for
Saltwater Fly Rods

The Seamaster
comes in two sizes

FLYCASTING LEADERS

Tapered saltwater leaders with 12-pound tippets are tied to the end of the line. For large fish, attach a 12-inch 80- or 100-pound "Shock" tippet to the end of the leader.

As is true for freshwater fly-fishing, saltwater is most effective on fish that feed in shallow water, such as weakfish (seatrout), striped bass, bonefish, channel bass (redfish), and snook. Though fly-fishing may at first seem an impractical method for catching fish weighing upwards to 20 or 30 pounds, many adept fly anglers have taken tarpon and billfish that weighed upwards to 150 pounds.

SALTWATER FLYCASTING ARTIFICIALS

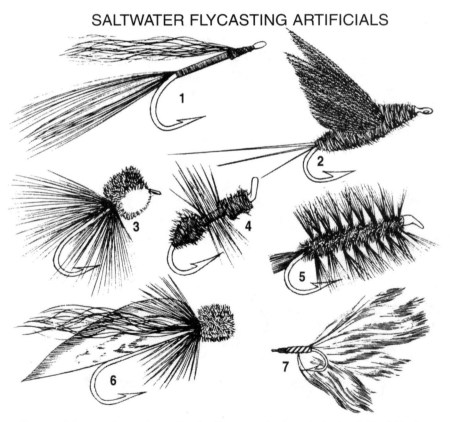

Seven of the most popular saltwater flies are displayed above: 1. Keel Hook Fly, 2. Fanwing (dry), 3. Bubble Pup, 4. Ant, 5. Woolly Worm (wet), 6. Mudder Minnow, 7. Marabou.

40

BOTTOM-FISHING

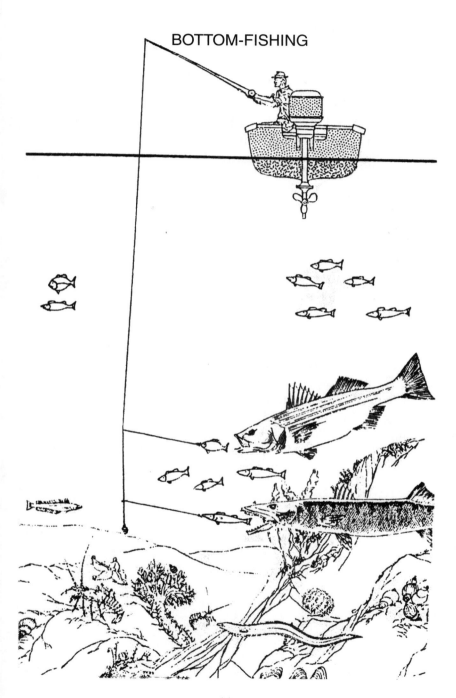

BOTTOM-FISHING RODS

Bottom-fishing is done from shore, bridges, piers, small boats, large boats, private boats, and charter and party boats. Most of the bottom-fishing rods are referred to as "pier" or "boat" rods. They range from about 5 to 7 feet in length and are made of solid or hollow fiberglass. The hollow or tubular rods are lighter than solid fiberglass.

For light bottom-fishing in shallow and protected bays, sounds, rivers, and inlets for small or medium-sized fish, the shorter, lighter bay rods can be used. They are about 5 to 6 feet long and have limber tips. You use them with smaller saltwater reels, lighter lines, and sinkers up to 2–4 ounces.

For general bottom-fishing from shore, piers, and boats, a rod about 6 or 7 feet long is best. Those with a light or limber action can be used with light lines and sinkers for small fish. But for large fish in deep water, or when fishing in strong currents or tides around rocks and wrecks, a heavy action rod is better. It must be able to handle sinkers up to 10 ounces.

Some anglers also use surf rods and reels, spinning rods and reels, and even some of the trolling or offshore rods. Surf rods, for example, are often used when fishing from piers or even boats, when casting is required. Saltwater offshore trolling or big game rods are used to catch big grouper or black sea bass.

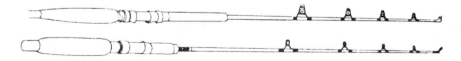

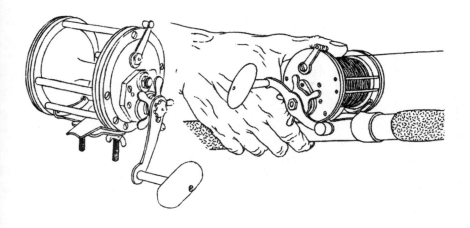

BOTTOM-FISHING REELS

Reels used for bottom-fishing are usually the conventional "pier" and "boat" saltwater models; these work well with most of the lighter bottom rods. But when you are using the heavier bottom-fishing rods for big fish in deep water, you often need larger reels. Here, many fishermen use conventional surf reels and the smaller "trolling," "big game" or "offshore" reels. Sizes No. 3/0, or 4/0 are the most popular since they hold more of the 30-, 40-, 50- and even 60-pound test lines needed. Most of the bottom-fishing reels have a metal spool, drag or brake, and free-spool lever.

BOTTOM-FISHING LINES

Years ago bottom fishermen used mostly linen lines, then they changed to braided nylon and Dacron lines. Some anglers still like to use Dacron lines when fishing in deep water because they have less stretch. But most anglers bottom-fishing today use monofilament lines. These are smaller in diameter, strong, and are less visible to the fish. When fishing for smaller fish (up to 4 or 5 pounds), you can use lines testing from 10 to 20 pounds. For larger fish (up to 20 or 30 pounds), use lines testing from 20 to 30 pounds. And for still bigger bottom fish over coral reefs or wrecks in deep water, use 40- to 50- and even 60- to 80-pound test lines.

HOOKS

Hook patterns used for bottom-fishing will depend on the species you are going after, and hook sizes will be governed by the size of the fish running in the area. One of the most popular hooks for bottom-fishing is the "claw" or "beak" type hook which has a rolled-in offset point. The old-time Sproat hook is still popular for small and medium sized fish such as sea bass, porgies, sheepshead, croakers, spot, perch, rockfish, and similar species. The Carlisle hook is a long-shank pattern which is good for fish that swallow bait or have sharp teeth. Use it for eels, flounder or fluke, small bluefish, and silver hake or whiting. Another old-time favorite is the O'Shaughnessy pattern, which is forged or flattened to give it strength. It can be used for large bottom fish such as cod, pollock, grouper, halibut, cabezone, and lingcod. Then there are specialized hook patterns such as the Chestertown, which is used for flounders, and the Virginia, used for blackfish or tautog and sheepshead. You can buy hooks already tied on snells or short leaders, and on rigs. They also come loose in a various quantities so you can tie your own leaders and rigs.

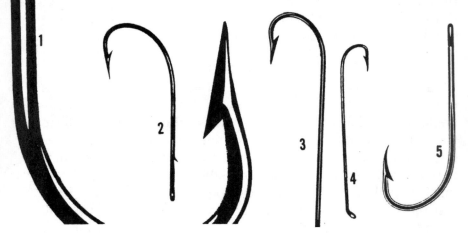

Popular hook types and sizes.
1. Mustad Shark Hook: sizes 6" to 1"; 2. Mustad Sproat Hook: sizes 6/0 to 3/0; 3. Superior Carlisle: sizes 10/0 to 20; 4. Mustad Hollow Point Flounder Hook: sizes 2 to 10; 5. Mustad Beak Hook: sizes 9/0 to 6,8,10,12. (More hook types and sizes on page 45.)

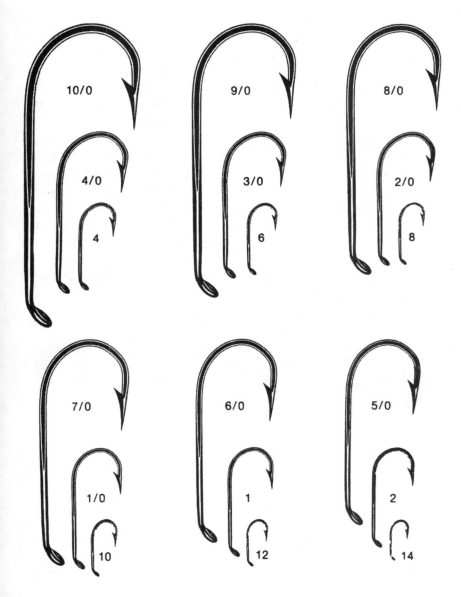

This page displays hook sizes ranging from 14 (very small) to 10/0 (medium large). All are typical of similar sizes in most types, styles and models of hooks.

(The above display is adapted with permission from a chart prepared by O. Mustad & Son, Oslo, Norway.)

SINKERS

Sinkers are very important in bottom-fishing because they get the bait and rig down to the bottom and either hold it there or let it bounce along the bottom. The most popular salt-water bottom sinker is the bank type, which is a long, narrow sinker with several side sides and an eye. It comes in weights of ½ ounce up to 16 ounces. The diamond sinker is a flat type of weight which is popular with bottom anglers going after fish in deep water. The ball or round sinker is a good one to use when fishing on bottoms covered with rocks since it doesn't get hung up as often as other types. The egg sinker is also good for rocky bottoms or coral reefs. It has a hole running through the center and slides up and down the line. To keep it away from the hook you tie on a barrel swivel, between line and leader, to act as a stop. You can also use pyramid sinkers for bottom-fishing over sandy bottoms; they are specially popular in surf fishing.

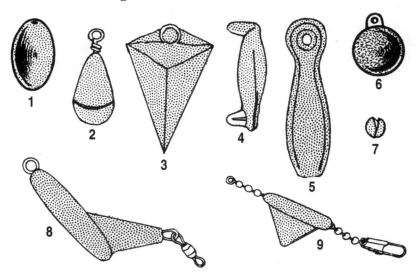

Displayed above are some of the sinkers which are used for fishing on the bottom: 1. The Egg sinker, 2. Dipsey, 3. Pyramid (sand sinker), 4. Clinch, 5. Bank, 6. Ball, 7. Split-shot or Buckshot.

These two sinkers are used exclusively for trolling: 8. The Drail, and 9. The Keel. Each is designed to offer the least amount of water resistance.

BOTTOM RIGS

A basic bottom rig has one hook on a short leader tied to a three-way or crossline swivel on the line. This hook can be tied just above the sinker or a foot or more above it, depending on the fish you are seeking. A variation of the one-hook rig is the two-hook bottom rig. Here you tie the first hook near the sinker, and a second hook high enough to clear the first (as illustrated). You can also make a four- or five-hook rig.

POPULAR BOTTOM-FISHING RIGS

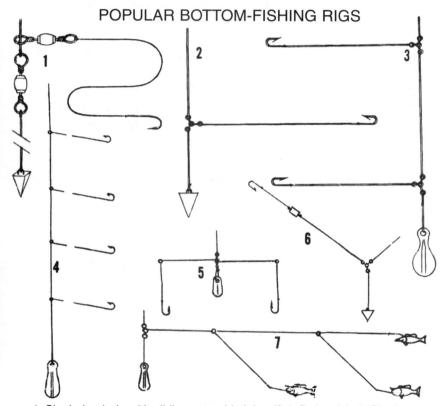

1. Single-hook rig with sliding pyramid sinker (fish finder rig), 2. Single-hook rig with pyramid sinker, 3. Two-hook rig for baiting bottom and above bottom-feeding fish, bank sinker, 4. Four-hook rig usually used for mackerel, for which the rig is named, 5. Spreader rig, often used for flounder fishing, 6. Floater, one-hook rig, often used with a small block of cork on the hook leader or snell to lift the bait above the bottom, ideal for live and dead bait, 7. Dropper bait rig that has two or more hooks tied into the main hook leader or snell, dropper fashion, used with live or dead small bait fish.

NATURAL BAITS

Bottom-fishing anglers usually use natural baits, which can be purchased at tackle and bait stores, marinas, and fish markets, or you can to catch your own. Seaworms such as clamworms, sandworms, pileworms, and bloodworms can be used to catch a great variety of fish. So can various kinds of clams found along the Atlantic and Gulf coasts. Strips of squid catch many bottom fish, as do crabs of many species. Shrimp, both live and dead, are excellent bait for many species. Baitfish such as pinfish, sand eels, killifish, pilchards, and mullet are also good when dead or alive. Larger fish can be cut up into chunks, steaks, or strips for bait. Along the Atlantic and the Gulf coasts bottom-fishing is often done by "party boats," also called "drift boats." They sail from most large cities and towns along the Atlantic and Gulf Coasts and charge for a half or a full day of fishing. Rods, reels and bait usually are furnished. On the Atlantic coast, anglers catch sea bass, porgies, flounders, flukes, mackerels, bluefish and cod. On the Gulf Coast they also catch many species of snappers and groupers.

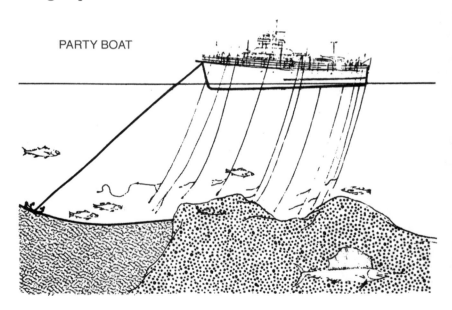

PARTY BOAT

48

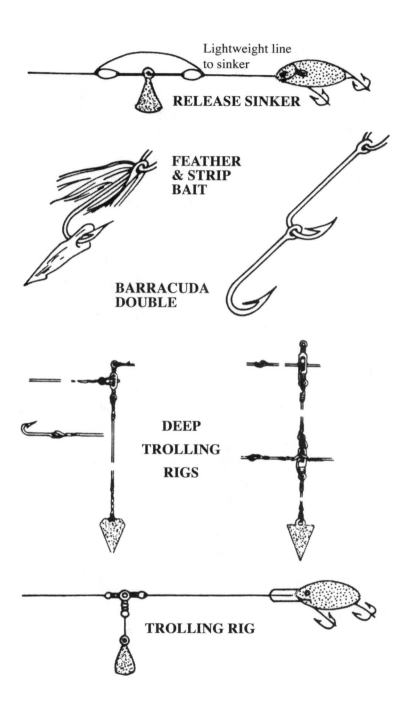

Lightweight line to sinker

RELEASE SINKER

FEATHER & STRIP BAIT

BARRACUDA DOUBLE

DEEP TROLLING RIGS

TROLLING RIG

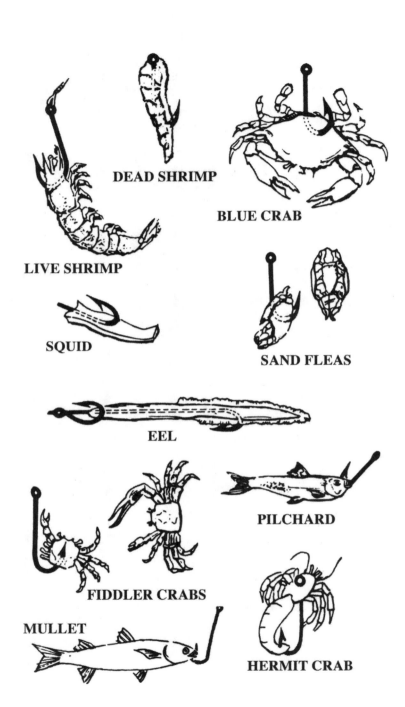

DEAD SHRIMP

BLUE CRAB

LIVE SHRIMP

SQUID

SAND FLEAS

EEL

PILCHARD

FIDDLER CRABS

MULLET

HERMIT CRAB

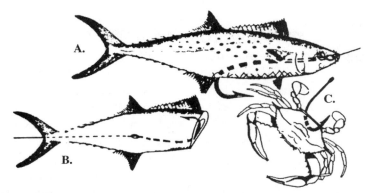

A. Whole fish rigged for trolling or drift fishing. Remove backbone for better trolling action. A second hook may be added in the anal cavity area.

B. Headless fish rigged for drift or bottom-fishing. (Hook may be added to the tail section.)

C. How to hook a blue crab.

D. How to cut fish for "cut-bait" for bottom-fishing. (Entrails and tail can be cut up for chumming.)

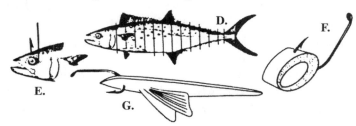

E. How to hook head of fish.

F. How to hook cut-bait.

G. Ventral or pelvic strip-bait for casting or trolling.

H. Squid hooked for trolling or drift fishing.

I. How to hook squid head for bottom-fishing. (Treble hook may be used by pushing hook shank and eye up through the mouth area in center of tentacles.

J. Eel rigged for casting or trolling. (Hook may be added in anal cavity area.)

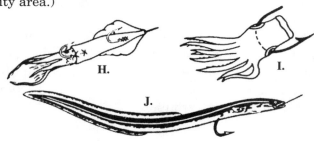

WHERE TO BOTTOM-FISH

Anglers must remember that bottom-feeding fish congregate only in areas where they can find food, shelter, and water temperatures to their liking. Bottom-fishing can be done almost anywhere from which the angler can lower or cast a bottom-fishing rig; pier, bank, surf, bridge, jetty, rocky shore, or from a boat anchored close to the shoreline or offshore.

One of the best areas for bottom-fishing is a broken or rocky bottom where sea worms and crustaceans are available, as well as many kinds of bait fish. Rocky bottoms are usually a hang-out for snappers, porgies, sea bass, amberjacks, and groupers. There are also many so called "banks" found in saltwater. These are in the form of submerged plateaus or shoals.

Shellfish beds of mussels, oysters and clams are also good places for bottom-fishing, as are artificial and natural reefs. The latter may be either in deep or shallow water, but those that are exposed during a low tide should be fished during, and for one hour after, the incoming high tide.

Breakwaters and jetties also offer good feeding grounds for bottom-feeders. Rocks of jetties are often covered with many forms of crustaceans which are favored by sheepshead, redfish, black drum, etc. Always lay your baited rig alongside the rocks or, if possible, lower it into a large hole between the rocks.

The pilings (wood or concrete) which support bridges, docks and piers are usually covered with oysters, barnacles and other mollusks and crustaceans. Dropping your baited rig off of these structures will often reward you with porgies, grunts, snappers, sheepshead and an occasional cobia or snook.

Offshore, in deeper water, can be found some of the best bottom-fishing grounds, especially over submerged wrecks, rocky bottoms, reefs, and seaweeds. Reefs and rocky bottoms are where many bottom-feeders find food and shelter. A baited rig dropped among these fish attractors will usually result in an immediate strike from barracuda, or an excellent tasting yellowtail snapper or grouper.

LOCATING BOTTOM-FISHING GROUNDS: A proven method for finding an ideal bottom-fishing area is to drift your boat with a baited rig bouncing along the bottom. When you get a bite or a fish, keep drifting over the area or lower the anchor and fish the spot.

A good bet for attracting fish close to your baited rig is to fill a mesh bag with "chum": ground, cut-up or chopped fish or other sea animals (crabs, clams, oysters, squid, etc.). In lieu of a mesh bag, you can build a small chum cage using wire mesh fence material; just make sure that the mesh is not so large that it allows ground or chopped chum to drift out of it. Whatever you choose, bag or cage, be sure to lift it up and down off the bottom occasionally so that the seafood oil can escape. The odor of this oil is what attracts the fish.

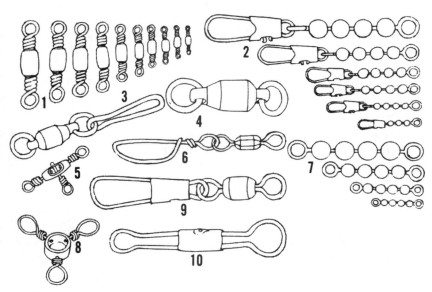

Some examples of the important pieces of equipment now being used by both fresh- and saltwater anglers: 1. Assorted barrel swivels, 2. Bead chain snaps, 3. Link snap swivel, 4. Big game ball bearing, 5. 3-way barrel swivel, 6. Coast-lock snap, 7. Bead chain swivels, 8. 3-way ring swivel, 9. Common snap w/swivel, 10. Connector.

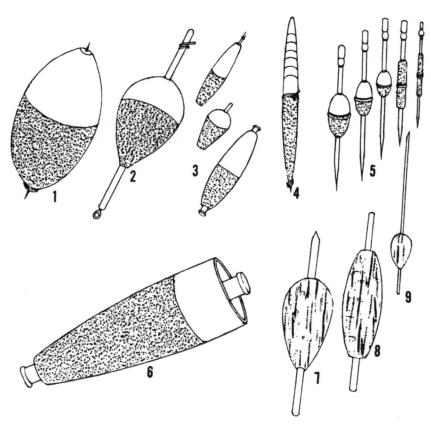

Floats commonly used by fresh- and saltwater anglers: 1. Casting, 2. Egg (bicolor), 3. Perch (3 kinds), 4. Hollow quill, 5. Panfish (5 kinds) 6. Popping, 7. Egg (natural), 8. Barrel (natural), 9. Stick-up.

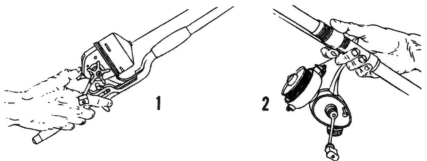

Two popular spinning reels: 1. Closed-face pushbutton type, 2. Open-face type. Both types perform equally as well for bait-casting and bottom-fishing.

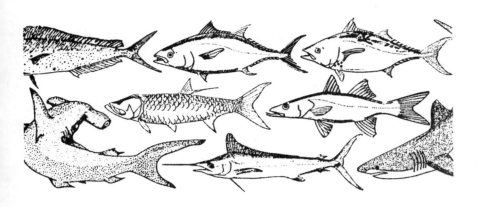

SALTWATER FISH AND HOW TO FISH THEM

There are literally thousands of fish species in our oceans. Used to great unobstructed spaces, many of them range widely and certain ones are pelagic, appearing along each portion of our coasts only at certain times of the year. As in freshwater, most of the species serve as forage for the fewer large species.

It would be impossible to cover all saltwater species in a book of this size. Only those species most popular with anglers are described here. Other species are caught while the angler is directing his endeavors toward a special favorite.

The more popular saltwater species may be put (somewhat arbitrarily) into the following classes: big gamefish, general gamefish, bottom fish. These groups greatly overlap, and even more than in freshwater angling, methods greatly overlap also.

BIG GAMEFISH: Many species of fish are recognized among saltwater anglers and the International Game Fish Association (IGFA) as being big gamefish. Some are extremely large while others, though much smaller, are real fighters on rod and reel. These large gamefish inhabit open oceans and for one to pursue them successfully, one must invest a considerable amount of money in tackle and guide service. For those who care to test themselves in battle against some of the most powerful of hook-and-line fishes, they are in for the thrill of a lifetime.

Species-wise, these large gamefish are not abundant, but they offer the sport angler the best of the world's marine heavyweight class.

Newcomers who want to try open-water fishing should first charter a boat to find out if they want to purchase their own saltwater tackle. In addition, the skipper and crew of a chartered vessel are a valuable resource for information. If the cost of the charter is more than you care to spend, join a party of anglers and just pay your share, or gather a group of your own angling friends, neighbors, and co-workers. Most popular sportsfishing ports have at least one large party boat in operation that makes daily trips to offshore or bay fishing grounds on a come-one-come-all basis. This is also a good way to get the opportunity to pay less, meet a lot of experienced anglers. The captain, guide and crew can help you to rig tackle (often supplied, either included in the price or for an additional charge). Bait, of course, is always furnished by charter boats.

In many ports, boats are available which can be boarded at night. On these, you rent a bunk and sleep while the boat runs out to offshore fishing grounds. A steward wakes you, you are served breakfast and fishing commences. Tackle is available at a cost that is seldom prohibitive for the average angler. Some of these boats furnish both trolling and bottom-fishing tackle, and anglers fish with a rotation system so each angler gets a chance at the best, or stern, position. In some ports, offshore anchored barges are available. A speedboat taxi service runs you to the barge and planned return trips are made at regular intervals. On the barge, food and tackle can be purchased. You may use your own rod or rent one.

If you plan to buy your own tackle (rod, reel, and the works), I suggest that you buy a surf outfit that easily can be used along the beach, from a bridge, pier, jetty or boat. The cost, whatever it may be, will be well worth it.

FISH IDENTIFICATION

For proper identification of a fish it is necessary for the angler to learn the superficial structure of a fish. Coloration is only one key to making a positive identification, and it is far from definitive. Individuals of the same species taken from different environments may differ in color. A good example is the snapper family; in particular, the dog snapper may have a background color of silver-gray, or copper, or brown, blended with red. Some specimens may be barred, others not. Also, all fish, after being caught and removed from the water, will show a rapid color change. A kingfish, when first caught, will have a dark greenish dorsal area, with silver-white sides and belly. But after just five minutes on a stringer it begins to darken all over, and by the time of death it attains an overall darkness that would make it impossible to identify by color alone.

Therefore, taking all methods of identification into consideration, my personal feeling is that the outline of a specimen is the only method of positive identification of the species. All outlines of the artwork of fish throughout the book are accurate enough to enable the angler to compare and identify a catch properly. For further identification a count of fin spines

Pompano, jack crevalle and blue runner are very similar in body shape and size. One way to distinguish them is by observing the number, size and shape of their dorsal fin spines.

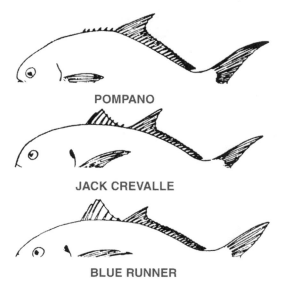

POMPANO

JACK CREVALLE

BLUE RUNNER

57

of the first and second dorsal fin will further the accuracy. For instance, the common jack, blue runner, and the pompano are very often mistaken for one another, especially when mixed schools of these fish are feeding together. However, if the angler will examine the spinous dorsal fin (first fin), separation is quite easy (see illustration.)

NAMES OF FISHES

Some species of fishes may have as many as five dozen common or angler's pet names. The names used in this book are the common names of the species that were selected by the American Fisheries Society, using input from the International Game Fish Association.

EXTERNAL ANATOMY OF A BONY FISH

RED DRUM (also known as redfish, channel bass, spot tail, red bass, red horse, school drum, puppy drum, among other common names.)

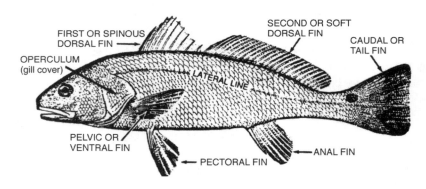

SECOND OR SOFT DORSAL FIN
CAUDAL OR TAIL FIN
FIRST OR SPINOUS DORSAL FIN
OPERCULUM (gill cover)
LATERAL LINE
PELVIC OR VENTRAL FIN
PECTORAL FIN
ANAL FIN

BIG GAMEFISHES

Big gamefish of the heavyweight class are herein described, as are their habits, habitats, their natural foods, and the most popular ways to fish for them. Stout heart, heavy tackle, and a little luck are required of the successful saltwater angler.

MARLINS, SAILFISHES AND SWORDFISHES are collectively known as "billfish." Marlins and sailfish belong to the same family, but the swordfish is in a family by itself. The long extension of the bill is round in marlins and sailfish, and flattened like the blade of a sword in the swordfish. Large swordfish have been known to ram a boat. In one particular incident, a swordfish drove its sword through planks that measured four inches thick. When hooked, billfish will often surge from the sea in leap after leap, shaking violently as they try to free themselves from the hook. An angler's fight with a sailfish may last for as much as an hour, while the battle with a large marlin may last two hours or more. A large swordfish is capable of keeping the most experienced angler busy for as much as a half of a day, depending of course, on the weight of the fish and the stamina of the angler. A large swordfish can tip the scales at 1,000 pounds or more. During a fight all billfish alternately leap into the air and bore deep into the water.

COMPARISON OF BILLS AND DORSAL FINS AMONG
SWORDFISH, SAILFISH, AND MARLINS.

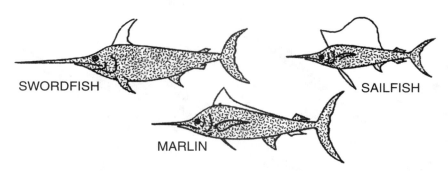

SWORDFISH

SAILFISH

MARLIN

One method of distinguishing these three fishes is by their dorsal fins. If the fin is high and about the same height as its full length, it belongs to a sailfish. If the fin is highest in front, the fish is a marlin. And if the fin consists of a single tall lobe, the fish is a swordfish. Of the marlins, there are three separate species, the blue marlin, the striped marlin and the white marlin. White marlin live in the Gulf of Mexico and are abundant in the Atlantic as far north as Massachusetts. The white marlin is the smallest of the three, weighing up to 150 pounds. The blue marlin averages 200 to 400 pounds, with a top weight of about 2,000 pounds. It is found in the same territory, but is more common in the Caribbean. Many also occur off the coast of Europe and Africa. One individual taken on rod and reel weighed 1,376 pounds. The swordfish is found worldwide in temperate and tropical oceans. This fish is also called broadbill or broadbill swordfish. It inhabits Continental

60

Shelf waters from the surface to depths of 400 to 500 fathoms (one fathom equals six feet). Spawning takes place in cool, deep waters, usually near submarine canyons or deep coral banks. The dorsal and pectoral fins of the swordfish are rigid and non-retractable, and a very large keel is present on each side of the caudal peduncle. Adult swordfish lack scales and do not have ventral fins. Coloration of the back may be dark brown, bronze, dark metallic purple, grayish blue or black. The sides may be dark like the back, or dusky; the lower sides of the head and belly may be dirty white or brownish-white.

Mentioned earlier was the attack by a swordfish which drove its bill through four-inch plank of a boat. In another incident, a swordfish attacked the Woods Hole Oceanographic Institution's submersible *Alvin* as it cruised at a depth of 330 fathoms. The fish wedged its sword so tightly into a seam that it could not withdraw it.

The natural foods of the swordfish include fish and squid. The fishing method most often used is trolling, when swordfish are spotted close to the surface, or deep drift fishing, especially at night. In either method of fishing, squid is most often used as bait. However, all kinds of deepwater fish (mackerel, dolphin, small tuna, bonito, eel and mullet). For best results when fishing the surface, clip your line to an outrigger that skitters the bait near or on the surface.

Swordfish often bask on the surface with their rigid dorsal fins protruding from the water. This habit makes them vulnerable to harpooners, who together with longliners (hook-and-line commercial fishermen) account for most swordfish catches. Among sportsfishermen, the swordfish is a coveted prize—difficult to locate, difficult to hook, and difficult to land because of its tremendous fighting ability. The swordfish is also an important commercial species. Its light colored, firm flesh has a unique and delicious flavor.

Swordfish are very finicky, easily frightened by approaching boats, and will rarely strike blindly. The bait must always be presented carefully, sometimes repeatedly, before the fish will take it. Because swordfish have soft mouths, hooking is one is an uncertain proposition, and the swordfish's long, slashing bill can make short work of the angler's line or leader.

When trolling for swordfish, the speed of the boat should be slowed when one is spotted (but not too drastically), and the bait should be eased quietly and gently in front of the fish. Once hooked solidly, the fight is on. It is said among big game-fish anglers that to land a swordfish is the highest achievement in angling.

THE MARLINS: The three species of marlins are among the world's greatest gamefish, as they are spectacular leapers and vicious fighters. They very rarely take artificial lures, but some success has been achieved using large bucktails. Most marlins are fished from guided charterboats, by trolling and using outriggers to skip or skitter the natural bait along the surface. Best baits include whole mullet, squid, dolphin and bonito. Sometimes strip bait is used, as well as a whole flying-fish or Spanish mackerel. The usual action that takes place during a strike is the marlin's habit of hitting the bait with the bill, to kill it, then turning and grasping it in the mouth. Therefore, this "bill tap" is felt first. The bait is then allowed to stay in the area of the tap, by releasing the brake on the reel. This allows the bait to drop back some distance on slack line, so that the bait will appear dead or injured, and will hang suspended or gradually sink below the surface. The marlin will slowly circle and seize the bait. At this time the angler quickly puts on the reel brake and sets the hook hard, and the fight is on. Should the angler miss, he should begin trolling immediately and try again.

Tackle for marlin must be heavy, and the angler should wear a shoulder harness and a rod-butt holder. The rod should be of good quality, as should the reel; 10/0 to 16/0 will do the job. A 25-foot long, No. 12 cable-type wire is usually preferred, because a marlin's giant leaps are not likely to kink it.

The white marlin, the smallest of the three, is generally much smaller than the blue and striped species. However, they are included here among the big gamefishes because of their fighting ability.

The white marlin has a blue-green dorsal area, grayish vertical stripes, and a silvery belly. It resembles a small blue marlin and inhabits the Atlantic Ocean and the Gulf of Mexico, preferring offshore waters of Florida in spring and moving farther north during summer. It sometimes travels in small schools. Average weight is about 100 pounds.

SAILFISH: There are two species of sailfish, the Atlantic sailfish and the Pacific sailfish. The Atlantic species ranges from Florida and Texas to New York, and the Pacific species ranges throughout most of the Pacific coast to Monterey, California. Distribution of sailfish is believed to be worldwide, but there is still some doubt about whether there is actually only one species of sailfish, or several closely-related species. One thing is for sure, those caught in the Pacific Ocean are much larger, on average, than those caught in the Atlantic.

Like the marlins, the sailfish is one of the fastest of all saltwater fishes, and speeds up to 60 knots have been reported, though most boat captains and crews consider 20 to 30 knots to be more representative.

The sailfish has a long, slender, vertically-compressed body that tapers evenly towards the deeply forked tail. The upper jaw is prolonged into a circular, needlelike bill. The main characteristic is its dorsal fin which is high and about the same height as its fun length. The peduncle, or tail stalk, has a double keel. Pelvic fins are long and retractable, and there are two small anal fins and two free-moving pectoral fins.

Coloration includes a dark blue or bluish-purple dorsal area. Flanks and belly have yellowish-gray hues, sometimes adorned with bluish-gray vertical bars composed of blue patches or spots. When opened, the sail is dark slate-gray or dark blue, with the membrane displaying a scattering of black spots. Average weight is about 65 pounds, but Pacific sailfish weighing 200 to 240 pounds have been caught. The function of the large, sail-like dorsal fin is not yet clearly understood, but it may assist in maneuvering.

Although sailfish are renowned as a sportfish and are capable of spectacular aerial acrobatics, they tire quickly.

Many anglers enjoy the fight much more when they use light tackle. Natural baits include flyingfish, needlefish, anchovies, squid and octopus. Anglers often troll large feathered jigs, bucktails, strip bait, or whole mullet, Spanish mackerel, bonito, or squid. Trolling with an outrigger is the best means of skipping or skittering the bait on the surface of the water. As in marlin and swordfishing, once a tap from the bill is felt, the bait is allowed to drop back. If there is no response, the bait should be put back into action immediately. Sometimes a second tap occurs, thus indicating a fish that would otherwise have been missed. Patience is a virtue! The usual action that takes place during a strike is like that of the marlins. Their habit is to hit the bait with the bill to kill or stun it, then turn and grasp it in the mouth to swallow it. Therefore, when the first tap is felt, release the reel brake and wait for a second tap or a "hit-and-run." Put on the brake and simultaneously set the hook hard and deep.

Sailfish are usually caught in distant offshore waters. Most are caught along the Texas Gulf Coast and along both Florida coasts, usually in the warm waters of the Gulf Stream. The most productive months are January to midsummer. Trolling from charter boats, using the same bait that is used for marlin, and handled it in the same manner, is the way to go.

GAMEFISH IN GENERAL: The gamefish presented here are considered by saltwater anglers to have top-notch sport qualities, and though a few of them require the use of a charter boat and guides, many can be taken from small boats rather close inshore with inexpensive tackle. In fact, a great number of them can be caught from bridges, piers, jetties and surf. For the most part they are "every angler's fish," and include some of the fastest and best fighters. Most are of good table quality. The rest are ideal for sport, and once the fight they give has been savored, they should be released for others to enjoy. For convenience to the reader, the following fish are not listed according to families, but instead are listed alphabetically by common name.

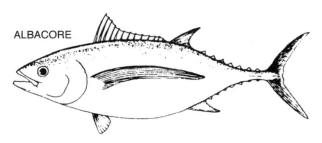

ALBACORE

ALBACORE: Range includes Atlantic and Gulf of Mexico off the Florida coast; uncommon farther north. In the Pacific it is abundant off the southern portion of California. The albacore is often mistaken for a small tuna, into which family it belongs. However, the characteristics that separate it from the true tunas are the pectoral fins, which on the albacore are extremely long, being almost half as long as the entire fish. The albacore lacks the stripes and spots on the lower flanks that are present on the true tunas, and the albacore has a white trailing edge on the margin of the tail fin. Lastly, the deepest part of the albacore's body is near the second dorsal fin, rather than near the middle of the first dorsal fin, as in true tunas.

The albacores is a fast swimmer. Its dorsal fins fit into slots on its backs so that they create no friction when the fish is traveling at top speed. To give an idea of its movement and speed, consider that an albacore tagged by biologists off the coast of California was caught two weeks later by commercial fishing persons near Japan; this would have required it to travel about 400 miles per day.

Millions of pounds of albacore are harvested every year off the western coast of the United States. Tremendously large schools appear in offshore waters in early summer and may still be present in the fall. Schools of smaller fish appear first, then the heavyweights.

Fishing methods for albacore include trolling with feathered jigs, or spoons. Live bait such as mullet, sauries, herring, sardines, anchovies, and other small fishes is used, as well as squid. Strips of mullet or Spanish mackerel are also good. Trolling at fast speeds is the key. When an albacore hits the bait, set the hook hard and then be ready for action, as it is a hard-fighting fish that will take the bait deep down. When it stops running or diving, begin "pumping" it up to the boat. Average weight is about 15 pounds, to a maximum of about 70 pounds.

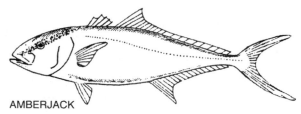

AMBERJACK

AMBERJACK: These fish are encountered in the Atlantic Ocean north to the Carolinas and in offshore waters off Florida in the Gulf of Mexico. This fish is a popular sport fish but many anglers do not eat them. However, their steamed flesh is unequalled in fish salad, and they are also delicious smoked. This large member of the jack family may grow to a length of 6 feet and weigh up to about 120 pounds. Amberjack travel in schools in tropical waters throughout the world. The amberjack is a powerful fighting fish that is pale bluish-silver with yellowish fins. A good field mark is the dark, olive-colored diagonal stripe that reaches from the mouth, across the eye to about the first dorsal fin.

To catch amberjack, troll around reefs using strip bait, feathered jigs, or large spoons. The amberjack is noted for its speedy runs into coral or other rocky places when hooked. Heavy tackle is the answer when pursuing this fish, because you must stop its powerful runs—otherwise you may lose your fish *and* your rig. A 6/0 reel spooled with 300 yards of 60-pound test, and a No. 8 wire leader with a No. 8 hook is adequate. When an angler catches the first amberjack, it is usually left on the hook and towed behind the boat, because others in the school often follow this decoy and are thereby hooked.

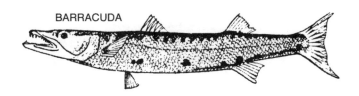

BARRACUDA

BARRACUDA: This fish occurs in all tropical seas except the eastern Pacific. It is found around reefs, wrecks, piers, and sandy and grassy flats. Large specimens are usually loners, while young barracuda often travel in schools. This fish should be regarded as a dangerous species because of its ability to inflict dangerous wounds upon a person, in or out of the water. Its bite is straight and clean.

Small barracuda give anglers great sport when hooked on light tackle, even a fly rod. However, large specimens may grow upwards to 90 pounds.

Coloration is bluish or dark on the dorsal area, silvery on sides and belly, with some indistinct dark spots. Natural foods consist mostly of fish, plus just about anything else that crawls or swims in the oceans.

Fishing methods for catching this fearless fighter include trolling, when the big ones are desired. To catch small specimens, bait casting or still-fishing in any area around reefs, and wrecks, both offshore and in areas around inlets and other protected areas, including small, deep lagoons. Using lightweight bait casting tackle to cast spoons and mullet strip-bait in bays and near-shore shoals often produces excellent results. A heavy saltwater fly rod using a large streamer, fished slowly, is also very good for small and medium-sized barracuda. In any type of fishing, a heavy wire, single-strand or braided leader is a must. As a food fish barracuda is questionable. I have eaten very small individuals, 1 to 2 feet in length, fried, and found them quite palatable. However, some people have gotten violently ill from eating barracuda, especially fish caught off Florida and Hawaii. The cause is ciguatera toxin, produced by a parasitic dinoflagellate that infects some fish. In California many restaurants include barracuda on their menus, but eating them is not nearly as enjoyable as catching them.

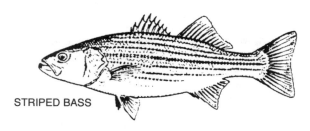

STRIPED BASS

BASS, STRIPED: Often called striper or rockfish, this species is by far the most sought-after surf-fishing target. It occurs from the St. Lawrence River to the Atlantic coast of north Florida, and in the Gulf of Mexico—Louisiana, Alabama and Mississippi, and along the U.S. Pacific coast from Washington to California. Although introduced relatively recently to the Pacific coast, on the east coast they have long been sought by saltwater anglers, and they have been one of the most important food fishes since the early 1600s. Striped bass move far upstream in rivers during spawning migrations. Their native freshwater range extends from the St. Lawrence River in New York, south to Florida's St. Johns River. In some of these waters, large populations have become landlocked due to artificial impoundments that blocked their return to the sea. In recent years the striped bass has been introduced into many freshwater lakes and rivers throughout the nation. In fact, the all-tackle record of 59 pounds 12 ounces was made in the Colorado River in Arizona.

Striped bass are easily recognized by the 7 or 8 prominent black stripes that run along the sides of the fish's long, silvery body, with one stripe running along the lateral line. It is a voracious and opportunistic predator that will consume all kinds of fish. Spawning takes place in fresh or brackish waters during the latter part of April on through early June.

Fishing methods vary. Saltwater fly rods are used, as are freshwater bait casting tackle, and heavy surf casting tackle. Many fish are taken by offshore trolling. Fly rod artificials include large and medium-sized streamers and other dry flies, as well as popping bugs like those used for largemouth bass. When bait casting, use largemouth or large pike plugs, spoons or pork rind. Large plastic worms and eels, as are feathered jigs. Any of the aforementioned lures can be used in saltwater or inland freshwater systems. However, to get the full feel of the fight, surf fishing is the best method. Most types of fishing for stripers are best employed during the early evening, through the night, and into the wee small hours of morning. Trolling near shore, especially around river mouths and small bays, using an eelskin rig, spoons, and spinners is equally effective day or night. Anyway you choose to fish, be sure to do it during an incoming tide, as this gives the best results.

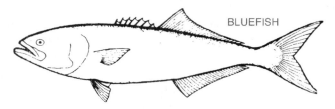

BLUEFISH

BLUEFISH: This fish is also called marine piranha, chopper, rock salmon, as well as about a dozen more regional names. Range includes the Gulf of Mexico and the eastern coastline of the Atlantic. The bluefish is a streamlined, elongated, blue-gray and silvery fish with a very deeply notched tail. Its mouth is filled with extremely sharp teeth, and the second dorsal fin has a very rigid sharp spine. This voracious fish has earned the nicknames "marine piranha" and "chopper" by swimming in schools along the beach and attacking swimmers and waders. Its feeding habit is nothing short of maniac, swimming as it does through shoals of bait fish, slashing and destroying everything in its path, including smaller fish of its own kind. The bluefish's bite can cause a nasty wound on a human, and the bite of a large individual can severe a finger or toe. As many careless anglers will attest, a bluefish can be dangerous when out of the water. It is very active and hard to hold while the hook is being removed. It is said that some anglers are capable of sniffing out bluefish by their smell, which is said to resemble cucumbers. (Herpetologists also sniff out the venomous copperhead snake, which is said to emit a similar odor.)

Several methods may be used to catch this battler, which is so greedy that it will strike at practically any moving lure.

69

Good natural baits include mullet, menhaden and squid. Artificials like bucktails, feathered jigs, spoons and spinners are also very effective. Many bluefish are caught in the surf using standard surf casting tackle. Inside waters, bays and mouths of brackish water inlets and outlets are excellent places to use sturdy bait and fly casting tackle. Surface and diving plugs, poppers and other largemouth bass and pike artificials are all good for the bluefish, as are streamers and other wet flies for the fly rod. For trolling, drift and still-fishing, use a hook size between 3/0 to 6/0. When still-fishing, chum with chopped Spanish mackerel or menhaden—the oilier the fish, the better. The baited hook is then drifted or cast into the oily slick on the surface of the water created by the chum. Weights may range from 1 to 25 pounds. The flesh of the bluefish has a tendency to become soft if it is not iced immediately and eaten as soon as possible. If time allows, clean and fillet a blue immediately after taking it from the water, after decapitating and allowing it to bleed. Bluefish will not keep for a long time, even when frozen.

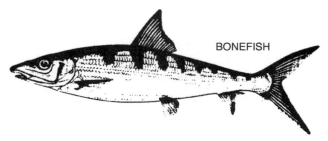

BONEFISH

BONEFISH: This fish was once very common in the Florida Keys. Anglers travel from all parts of the world to test their skill against bonefish. It occurs in shallow waters around flats and intertidal areas. It is a pale, brownish fish with silvery sides and belly; parts of the snout and fins display a yellowish or dusky color. Its structure is rather chunky, but also streamlined, with the mouth set far under, and an odd, overlapping, humped snout. Weights average 2 to 6 pounds, with a maximum of about 15 pounds.

Bonefish are schooling fish, and small ones are often observed in large schools on the flats. Larger individuals tend to form smaller schools. The bonefish feeds on all kinds of small fish, crabs, shrimp, clams, sea worms, and sand fleas. This fish is capable of giving an angler a lot of excitement when it is hooked on light or medium saltwater tackle.

Fish for bonefish around the Florida Keys during the spring and summer months, and in early fall. The wariness of this fish and the shallow water make "bonefishing" a challenge. It can be done wading or from a double-anchored skiff. Once the bonefish's feeding grounds have been located, the angler readies his tackle as soon as the high tide begins to move in, and waits for swirling or "tailing" fish. Bonefish are often seen rooting in the sand for mollusks, their tails breaking the surface of the shallow water. This action is known as "tailing." At other times they will plough the bottom, stirring up silt and marl. Such action is known as "mudding." Very often chum of shrimp, crab and clams is thrown out, along with the baited hook and a very light sinker (or no sinker) following. The bite of a bonefish is a slight tug as the fish mouths the bait. When the tug is felt, the angler should set the hook immediately. Fly rod fishing with heavy tackle using size 1/0 trout flies also can be a lot of fun. The fly is quietly cast very close to the feeding fish,using plenty of backing line on a large single-action reel. Bonefish are awesomely swift, strong, never-say-die fighters. They are solely fished for sport and should be released, being too bony to make good eating.

TUNAS: Tunas are members of the mackerel family, and are swift swimmers that travel in schools through warm temperate seas throughout the world. Among the tunas are some of the most famous gamefish in the world, and they are also important commercially.

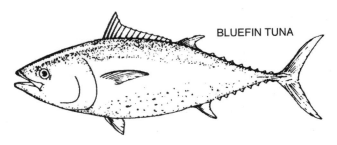

BLUEFIN TUNA

BLUEFIN TUNA: This is one of the largest fishes in the sea and is also the most sought-after tuna by sport anglers. When traveling, tuna will feed on small schooling fish that cross their path. Food include menhaden, Spanish mackerel, and flyingfish, among other species. The schools of small tuna are called "school tuna" by anglers and average 20 to 100 pounds. Really large tuna, those weighing from 200 to over 1000 pounds, are often referred to as "horse mackerel."

Bluefin tuna have a dark blue dorsal area, with flanks paling to grayish or silvery; belly and cheeks are silvery, dorsal fins are dusky blue-gray, and the dorsal and anal finlets are tinged with yellow. The pectoral fin is short, and the tail is crescent-shaped. Size varies with geographic area, with 1,000-pound individuals in some areas, while elsewhere specimens reach 14 feet in length and weigh up to 1,800 pounds.

Bluefins range along both coastlines, but the most famous fishing grounds are off Bimini, West Indies, during winter and spring, and New Jersey to Nova Scotia, summer and fall. The best fishing method is trolling along offshore banks and at tide rips. Chumming is a very important part of tuna fishing. Dropping chunks of herring and Spanish mackerel overboard is the usual procedure, with the hook, baited with whole herring or Spanish mackerel, drifting with the chum each time it is thrown overboard. In some areas drift or still-fishing while chumming brings excellent results. When tuna are schooling close to the surface, trolling with an outrigger is very effective when natural baits are used. The skipping and skittering of natural bait resembles flyingfishes, one of the main sources of food for all tunas.

Trolling for large tuna should only be done from a charter boat with an experienced captain and/or guide, and a good crew. Why? When a large bluefin is hooked, you are going to need all the help you can get. Playing a large tuna, with its tremendous strength, requires a captain who knows how to maneuver the boat to your advantage. A helpful crew member also comes in handy, to pour cold water over your hot reel and to be ready to render assistance, should the fighting chair break loose from the deck.

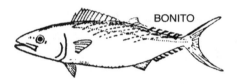

BONITO

BONITOS: These fish are shaped very much like tuna, to which they are closely related. Four species swim in Atlantic and Gulf waters, and all are noted for their speed, power and fighting ability when hooked. Coloration includes blue on the upper parts, with silvery and yellowish below. Dark stripes run the length of the body, but on a slight upward angle. The head is large and the body is torpedo-shaped. All four species are schooling fish. The striped bonito usually lives in large schools, in the open surface waters of the Atlantic and Gulf of Mexico, along the shorelines of Florida, Texas, Alabama, Mississippi, Georgia and the Carolinas, and northward to Massachusetts. The striped species averages between 15 and 20 pounds.

Most catches of bonito are accidental. They are usually caught while fishing for other surface-feeding fishes. For this reason, anglers should use medium to heavy trolling tackle; there is always a chance of tying into something bigger than what you're fishing for. Strip natural baits are good. Artificials such as feathered jigs and spoons are sometimes very rewarding. The flesh of the bonitos are not considered particularly tasty.

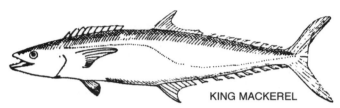

KING MACKEREL

KING MACKEREL: Also called "cero," this fish is easily distinguished from the bonitos by its high dorsal fin, slender form and spotted sides, and from small tunas by its color, and by its dorsal fins. Coloration includes a dark blue on the upper half of the first dorsal fin. Dorsal area is deep blue shading to silver on the the sides and belly, with rows of oval-shaped, yellowish-orange spots on the sides. These very popular small gamefish bring anglers out by the hundreds when they are running. Small ones are often used as bait for larger gamefishes. They are excellent as a table fish. Heavy commercial fishing for this species has depleted the population to such an extent that seasons are strictly regulated. Always check with the local bait shops for the latest rules governing king mackerel seasons and bag limits.

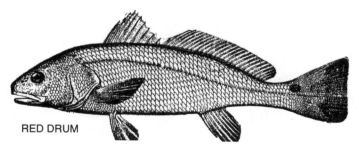

RED DRUM

RED DRUM: Also called channel bass, redfish, spot-tail bass, red bass, and many other regional names. This fish is found along the Atlantic coast from New Jersey to Florida and also along the coast of the Gulf of Mexico. Coloration includes an overall coppery tinge. The nose is blunt and the tail fin is square across the tip; belly is a coppery white. Coloration usually changes to brick red after death. This fish is easily recognized by its most outstanding characteristic, a black spot on each side of the tail, about the size of the fish's eye. Sometimes there are two or more spots, and they may appear on the body.

The red drum is a schooling fish that occurs inshore over mud or sandy bottoms. It inhabits both salt and brackish water and occasionally is found in freshwater lakes and rivers. Small fish feed in rivers, sounds, and inlets, while larger specimens feed in the surf and around pier and bridge pilings. Average weight is about 5 pounds, but fish weighing 10 pounds are not uncommon. The rod and reel record is 90 pounds. The redfish is a strong, hard fighter when hooked.

The preferred fishing method for large individuals is surf casting. For average-sized fish, piers, bridges, and bays are best. Both large and small specimens may be caught while drifting, still-fishing and slow trolling close to the shoreline. Shallow, sandy and grassy flats may be fished "bonefish style." Natural baits include crabs, shrimp, clams, sea worms, finger mullet, and sand bugs or fleas. Artificials can be weighted bucktails, feathered jugs, and streamer flies for the fly-rodder. Red drum weighing up to 15 pounds are good eating, though the meat of larger specimens may be a little coarse for some people.

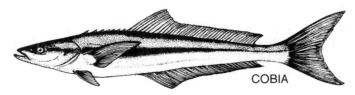
COBIA

COBIA: Also called crab-eater, this fish of Florida and Carolina waters is a long, dark-brown to cream-colored fish, solid as a mackerel, and a powerful fighter. It is considered a prize as a sportsfish, and a prize for the table. Its flesh is absolutely delicious whether baked, broiled or fried.

The cobia bears a striking resemblance to the remora (shark sucker), but it lacks the sucking discs on the top of the

75

head. The average weight of a cobia is less than 10 pounds, but a rod and reel record weighed 135 pounds and measured more than 5 feet in length.

As a gamefish, the cobia is highly rated as a hard-hitting fish with a lot of fighting spirit, and is prone to long, powerful, determined runs with a leap or two here and there. The cobia is not an easy fish to bring to the gaff; about half of those hooked are lost. Although large individuals are solitary, young ones usually travel in small schools and when one is hooked, other individuals are often observed swimming alongside it. Sometimes an entire group or school will surface with it. Cobia tend to hang around boat markers and buoys, as well as near the pilings of piers and bridges.

Methods of fishing include trolling with natural or artificial baits, bottom-fishing, drift fishing, and surf casting. The cobia's favorite foods include crustaceans, especially crabs of all kinds. This habit has given it the nickname "crab eater." It is not common anywhere, and most are caught by accident. Many are hooked by anglers fishing for spotted trout (weakfish) in weedy flats, and by anglers fishing for black drum around piers and bridges, the latter being a devoted crab-eater too. Ideal baits also include small fish, squid, strip or whole mullet, and shrimp.

DOLPHIN: This is one of the most beautifully colored of all gamefishes. The dolphin is so distinctive in body shape and color that it cannot be mistaken for any other fish. The male, or bull, has a high, straight forehead; the head of the female is also high but has a distinct upward slope to the dorsal fin. Coloration includes a mid-dorsal area of deep ocean blue, grading into green on the upper sides and yellow from the lateral line to the silver belly. The sides are sprinkled with a mixture of light and dark spots. The dorsal fin starts far forward, almost directly over the eyes, and extends back to the deeply forked tail; the anal fin is also long, stretching over about half the length of the body. The laterally-compressed body is streamlined, tapering sharply from head to tail. The dolphin is one of the fastest swimmers, and dashes upwards to 50 miles per hour have been authenticated. As many anglers will

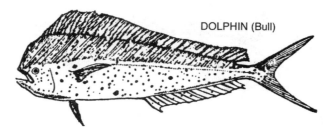
DOLPHIN (Bull)

attest, the run of a hooked dolphin will make your line sing as it is stripped from the reel. This fish ranges from the Gulf of Mexico to the Carolinas, and from California to Oregon. It is an open-ocean fish that feeds on all kinds of smaller fish, and is extremely fond of flyingfish. It may be a loner or travel in small schools. Weight averages about 5 pounds, with 20-pounders not being uncommon. Many have been caught that weigh in at as much as 50 pounds, and the record is somewhere around 85 pounds.

Methods of fishing include trolling with strip bait, (preferably from an outrigger), whole mullet or flyingfish, or with metal spoons or feathered jigs. Use light tackle for sport, or heavy tackle if you want to make sure that you bring some home for dinner. The trick of successful school-dolphin fishing is to tire the first one hooked, then keep it in the water, close to the boat without landing it. This method will usually hold the school together, and often others will be close enough for bait casting. Active anglers using this method have been known to clean out a school in short order. When hooked, a dolphin will often leap or tailwalk, darting first in one direction and then another. Runs are extremely fast and powerful, and high-test lines have been snapped by fish half the weight of the line-test. This usually happens when the brake is prematurely engaged, or the drag is changed while the fish is running.

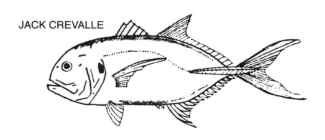

JACK CREVALLE

JACKS: There are several species of fish that are called "jacks." They are members of a family of fish that also includes the pompanos. Jacks are found in both Atlantic and Pacific, but are less common in the latter. The jack crevalle is very common in the Gulf of Mexico around Florida. This fish has a steep, blunt forehead, deep body, forked tail, and a lateral line that is deeply curved down toward the tail. It has bony plates along the caudal peduncle. Its body color is iridescent gray-blue and yellowish-gray. All jacks are swift, stubborn battlers. Offshore whoppers are usually taken while trolling for other fish; strip bait, spoons, feather jigs and the like are used. Surf fishing will sometimes catch large individuals, but the best jack fishing method is bait casting in bays, inlets, and channels, either from the shoreline or from a boat. Yellow feathers and plugs have proven to be the most effective. Jacks are not especially good for the table, but if fillets are removed along the liver line, the white flesh is very tasty. Steamed jack is hard to beat for salads and gumbos.

SNOOK: This large fish has a big mouth, two dorsal fins, and a narrow, dark stripe down the side. Its body is robust and slightly compressed. Its head is depressed, with scaly cheeks and a lower jaw that projects beyond the upper. Color is dark olive to bluish above, whitish below, with a conspicuous, narrow, black stripe along the lateral line. Snook attain weights of up to 50 pounds.

Snook are abundant around Florida. They feed on all kinds of small fish and shrimp. The places to fish for them are brackish-water rivers, inlets, mud flats, mangrove shorelines, sandy channels, and even those freshwater lakes and rivers that link to the fish's saltwater habitat. The snook is a bait caster's delight—it will smash into almost any artificial, sur-

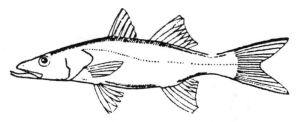

face, divers, or sinking lure. Fly-rodders will do well with large wet flies and streamers. Best fishing is at night around bridges, from piers, in the surf, or still-fishing with a lantern a little offshore. In elusiveness the snook is often compared with the northern freshwater fish, the muskelunge. Many anglers go forth in quest of these two fish, but very few catch a musky or snook.

Anglers landing a snook should be extremely careful when removing the hook, as the gill cover is serrated and as sharp as a razor. The snook is an excellent table fish with delicate, white, flaky meat.

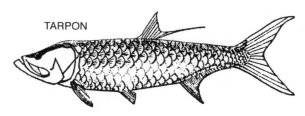

TARPON

TARPON: This large fish has very large, silvery scales, a deeply forked tail, large mouth, and with the last ray of the dorsal fin greatly elongated. Its body is compressed and the lower jaw juts out and up. Color is bluish-silvery above, silvery on sides and underparts. The tarpon is most abundant on Florida's central and southern coastlines. Its food includes all kinds of small fish, crabs and shrimp.

The tarpon is one of our greatest gamefish, a desperate fighter and a spectacular leaper. Its bony mouth makes it hard to set a hook, and its great leaps make it almost impossible to keep it hooked. Tarpon anglers usually comb the surface of the water for schools of rolling and feeding fish. Once tarpon are sighted, anglers troll slowly with natural bait (usually strip bait), artificial lures and spoons. Many anglers pre-

fer to still-fish with a live or dead mullet, or a whole blue crab, left lying on the bottom. Bobber fishing with pinfish and large shrimp is also effective. Hook sizes should be 9/0 to 11/0, leader a No. 9 about 6 feet in length. Plug casting with popping bugs when fishing for small tarpon in bayous and canals is very sporty also. When fly-fishing for this fish, nothing short of heavy equipment should be used, with plenty of line backing for the initial run and the up and coming leaps. Tarpon meat is bloody and mushy, not suitable for consumption. The tarpon is not a table fish and should be released when caught.

WAHOO: This fish is found worldwide in tropical and warm temperate seas. They are somewhat abundant in our waters off the Florida coastlines, mostly off the southern part of the peninsula and the keys. Wahoo are solitary, or travel in small groups. Color is blue or green above, silvery below. This fish has great speed and great fighting ability. It is a powerful fish with a heavily toothed mouth. It is solitary in deep waters of the open sea and along deep offshore reefs. Average weight is about 15 pounds, with a maximum of over 100 pounds. The preferred fishing method is trolling with strip bait, or spoons and feathered jigs. Wahoos are usually caught while trolling for dolphin, marlins, or sailfish. Wire leader is essential.

WEAKFISHES: Weak fishes or sea trouts include about 15 different species. They are found along the Atlantic and Pacific coasts of North America. All are slim-bodied and trout-like in appearance. The name weakfish applies to the tender mouths, from which hooks tear easily. Many anglers use landing nets when fishing from the shoreline or boat to keep from losing their catch. The common weakfish and the speckled seatrout are rather common in the surrounding waters of Florida. The speckled species is very popular among sport and recreational anglers. They are caught by bait casting or still-fishing while wading, either from the shoreline or from a boat. Shrimp is the best bait, though artificials used include all kinds of jigs. Grass flats are the best places to fish for them, although many are caught from piers and bridges. In an emergency this writer used a weighted hook and a strip of white cloth torn from a handkerchief, with much success.

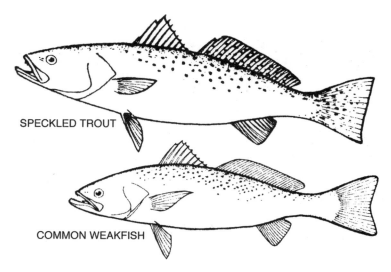

SPECKLED TROUT

COMMON WEAKFISH

Both species are olive to grayish above and have spots. However, the common species has small spots on the sides while the speckled seatrout has larger black spots that are scattered about the body, and also on the dorsal fins as well as the tail fin. All weakfish are considered fine table fish.

PACIFIC YELLOWTAIL: This is often called "amberjack," and it is shaped like its Florida relative the greater amberjack. Another species, the Florida yellowtail, is not related, but is a member of the Snapper family. In the Pacific species, the colors are separated by a light, lemon-yellow stripe running along the median line from tail to eye.

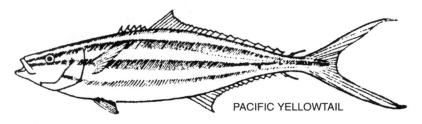

PACIFIC YELLOWTAIL

The Pacific yellowtail is a coastal schooling fish that stays close inshore around rocks, feeding on small school fish. It is one of California's top gamefish. It can be taken by surf casting, but is most often fished by trolling herring, sardines, or metal spoons with feathered jigs. Weight averages about 10 to 15 pounds, with a maximum of about 75 pounds. The Pacific yellowtail is a fast swimmer and its strike is vicious. When the fish hits the bait, allow slack in the line and time for the fish to swallow the bait before setting the hook hard.

BOTTOM FISH

Among the following described fishes are no gamefish, and they hardly qualify as sport fishes. However, all are very much fished for by recreational anglers and all are fun to catch and fine to eat. Many are caught while fishing in the surf for gamefish, while others are taken by still-fishing from the shoreline or a boat. Only the most popular and most important bottom fish are presented.

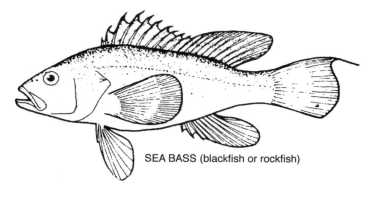

SEA BASS (blackfish or rockfish)

SEA BASS : Also called blackfish and rockfish, This is one of the most commonly caught fish by anglers who are bottom-fishing for groupers. Its range includes the western North Atlantic ocean, along the United States east coast from Massachusetts to the Gulf of Mexico. The black sea bass is, as a rule, a deep-water species that inhabits rocky bottoms and offshore reefs. However, many are caught by anglers fishing from piers with deep drop-offs, or by those that fish around wrecks and over shell beds. This fish can be caught throughout the year, but May, June, November and December are especially good times to fish for them. When hooked on light to medium saltwater tackle, the sea bass will fight all the way up to the surface; many anglers therefore consider it a gamefish. Color is grayish to black with indistinct mottlings or stripes. Natural foods include crabs, clams, small fish, etc. These also prove to be the best bait, but sea bass are also taken on fish chunks. As a food fish the flesh of the black sea bass is white and firm, and delicate in flavor.

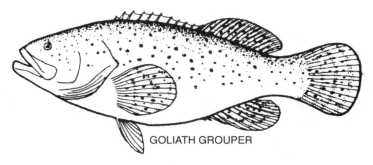

GOLIATH GROUPER

GOLIATH GROUPER: This fish is known as the California sea bass on the west coast, and was once called the spotted jewfish in the eastern U.S., but it is now known as the goliath grouper. It is a large fish with a huge mouth and a body that is dark in color, mottled with a lighter color than that of the background color. It feeds on rocky bottoms near jetties in deep waters, around wharves, and in inlets and channels. Although it prefers crustaceans, it also includes fish in its diet. It has been known to inhale a sea turtle into its enormous mouth. The goliath grouper is the largest member of the grouper family, attaining lengths of 8 feet and weights exceeding 700 pounds. Large specimens often live in underwater caves, and are very sluggish and protective of their domain. They are very curious and have been known to approach divers. Some have even attempted to swallow a diver, and there are some authenticated records where a huge fish had held divers by the arm, leg or head, in their large mouth, and caused their death by drowning.

Once a popular target of hook-and-line anglers and spearfishermen, goliath grouper now have become so scarce that they are protected by law. If you should inadvertently hook one, release it immediately.

GROUPERS: There are many species of grouper in both the Atlantic and Pacific oceans, but in the Atlantic they are most abundant offshore in the Gulf of Mexico. Their population thins north of the Carolinas. The groupers' body shape is very similar to that of largemouth bass. Grouper species include black, red, yellow, Nassau, and rock groupers, red hind, tripletail, etc. All are spotted or mottled. Natural foods

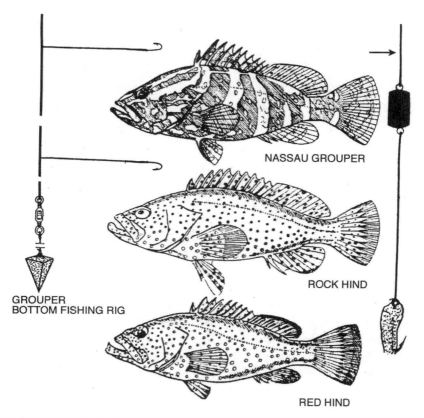

NASSAU GROUPER

ROCK HIND

GROUPER
BOTTOM FISHING RIG

RED HIND

include small fish, crabs, and shrimp. Average weight is 5 to 25 pounds, with a maximum of over 100 pounds.

Groupers are very popular among charter boats that go to grouper grounds far offshore in depths of 100 feet of water or more. They are caught by offshore trolling with strips of mullet attached to a spoon, or by still-fishing over deep, rocky reefs. They can be fished in bays and inlets, trolling with feather jigs, spoons, and plugs, or by still-fishing close to the bottom with chunk (cut) bait, and shrimp. Rods used should be of medium weight, with line of at least 40-pound test and about an 8/0 hook. Grouper run heavy and fight hard and deep, and must often be turned before they get a chance to run into rocks or other shelters. Groupers change colors quickly when taken from the water. All are excellent eating fish.

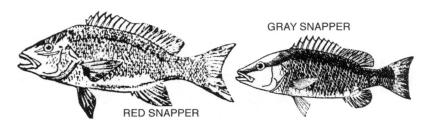

GRAY SNAPPER

RED SNAPPER

SNAPPERS: More than 250 species make up this important family of fish found in the warm seas throughout the world. Some are fished commercially, others are considered sport fishes. Snappers may be distinguished from groupers by their pointed pectoral fins. Their range includes offshore and coastal waters in the Atlantic and Gulf of Mexico, with the red snapper being the species most sought-after by commercial fishermen and sport anglers. Red snapper inhabit water 150 feet or deeper. Many are caught by anglers fishing from charter boats, with the boat's skipper using an electronic depth-finder to locate shoals of fishes. Once fish are located, the anchor is dropped and anglers use handlines or rod and reel to catch these excellent food fishes. Other popular snappers that are good sport and fine eating include gray (mangrove) snapper, lane snapper, schoolmaster, muttonfish, and dog snapper. All feed on or close to the bottom, most avidly at night, on all kinds of prey. Except for the red and a few other larger snappers, most snappers frequent both deep and shallow water. The gray snapper, a very popular fish among anglers, can be caught in three feet of water or less, especially around the mangroves, piers, bridges, and boat docks. Many of these good-tasting small fish can be caught in the surf and along shorelines. Most red snappers weigh about 5 pounds, but 20-pound catches are not uncommon. Occasionally fish weighing 30 to 40 pounds is taken, with the maximum being about 50 pounds.

Methods of fishing vary only slightly from one species to another. For deep-water red snapper, a handline or heavy tackle is needed to pull these prize fish from the great depths in which they live, using cut-up chunks of fish for bait. The other species of snapper seldom weigh more than about 4 pounds. The yellowtail snapper found in Florida waters looks

86

quite unlike the others. It has a forked tail, its color is grayish blue, silvery and pink, with a broad, yellow stripe that extends from the snout through the eye, and along the sides to the tail, above the lateral line. This particular snapper weighs up to 6 pounds and is usually solitary, often swimming 20 feet or more above the bottom, rather than hugging it as the majority of snappers do. The yellowtail is not only a good sport fish; it is equally as good on the table.

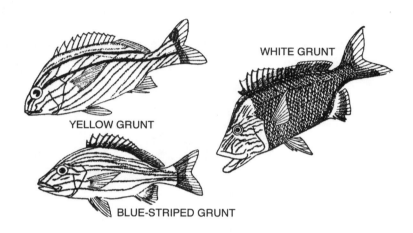

WHITE GRUNT

YELLOW GRUNT

BLUE-STRIPED GRUNT

GRUNTS: There are several hundred species of grunts that are abundant in the warm seas of the world. Their name is derived from the grunting noises they make when grinding their teeth. Most are small, deep-bodied fishes. Typically they travel in schools, and all are bottom-feeders. Grunts are plentiful in the Atlantic, inshore off the Carolinas and Florida. There are gray grunt, white grunt, yellow grunt, and pigfish. The latter is found north to New York, while the others are most abundant off the coast of Florida and in the Gulf of Mexico. Most members of this family of fishes are strictly bottom fishes, and many resemble freshwater sunfishes. Many have red mouth parts and most are good to eat.

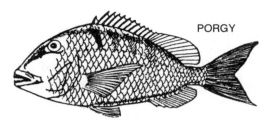

PORGY

PORGIES: This family of fish is very similar to the grunts, but in most porgies the body is even more flattened or compressed from side to side. They are medium-sized to small. Some live offshore while some others stay inshore. All may be used, whole and alive, for larger gamefish bait. Most are also good to eat. The northern porgy, found from the Carolinas to Maine, seldom weighs more than 2 pounds.

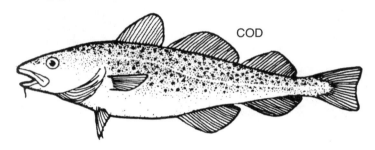

COD

COD: This fish ranges from North Carolina northward. It is a long, deep-bodied fish, somber brown to gray, with scattered dots. It is pale below, with a white lateral line. A chin whisker or barbel is present. This fish inhabits both deep and shallow water, depending on season. Foods include any marine animal that swims or crawls and will fit into its mouth. Cod are an important commercial food fish, but the fishery has collapsed from various causes and only recently has it started to recover. Weight of codfish averages 15 pounds, with a maximum of about 250 pounds. Anglers' catches average about 7 to 10 pounds for those caught in coastal waters, and 20 to 25 pounds offshore. Natural foods consist of small fishes, mollusks, crabs, and seaworms. Fishing deep around rocks, by handline with light to medium tackle baited with any of their natural foods will usually prove lucrative.

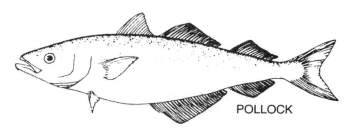

POLLOCK

POLLOCK: Of all the members of the cod family, the pollock is probably the most popular among anglers. Although found close to shore on both sides of the Atlantic Ocean, it is commercially netted in depths of 400 to 500 feet. It is greenish in color and runs in large schools, most often in deep, cold offshore waters. Deep, slow trolling with fairly heavy equipment, using spoons, jigs, and spinner baits works well, especially when used in combination with strip bait. Hook size should be around 9/0. Often, a school of pollock will feed on the surface. If you see this, troll slowly around the school, then slowly swing through it, bringing the bait into the school; this gets tremendous results. Small pollock are active feeders. Fish them with saltwater fly rod and tackle, using dry and wet flies and streamers. Still-fishing from a boat or in the surf is enjoyable, especially in deep bays; use crabs as bait. Average weights are from 4 to 10 pounds, but some offshore catches weigh more than 30 pounds.

BLACK DRUM: This fish ranges from waters off Massachusetts to Texas, in the Atlantic and in the Gulf of Mexico. It is a large-scaled, deep-bodied fish with chin whiskers or barbels. Its body is silvery gay with indistinct, dark, vertical stripes. The young are brilliantly striped, while

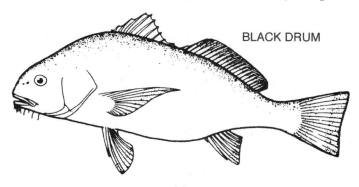

BLACK DRUM

89

mature specimens are essentially stripeless. Large, tough, sharp spines are present in the forward portion of the dorsal fin. Black drum feed primarily on crabs and mollusks, the shell or shells of the latter crushed by large throat teeth. In bays, fish for black drum over oyster beds or in the surf at high tide. Fiddler and other crabs, clams, and shrimp are good baits. Black drum rarely hit artificials, although jigging with a piece of shrimp will sometimes work. Large drum are fair eating, and small specimens are quite good.

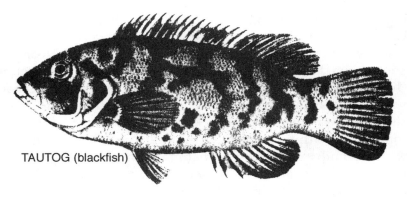

TAUTOG (blackfish)

TAUTOG or BLACKFISH: This fish ranges from the Carolinas north. It is a chunky, steep-headed, darkly mottled fish of rocky bottoms. It is found around bays, coves, and inlets, where it feeds on assorted shellfish. Its average weight is 2 to 5 pounds, with a maximum of about 20 pounds. It is usually caught by anglers still-fishing from small boats just offshore in about 20 to 30 feet of water, or while casting in the surf or fishing deep holes along rocky shorelines. Crabs and clams are the most popular natural baits. A hook size of 4/0 is the best. This is a good scraper that makes fine eating.

Young fish are usually brown or greenish-brown with irregular dark mottling or blotchiness on the flanks. Large specimens may be entirely black or charcoal gray, often with greenish overtones, or they may be mottled with brown, black, and white. The belly and chin are almost always white or gray, and sometimes there are spots on the chin. This fish's year-round availability, combined with large size and stubbornness when hooked, makes it a popular sport fish, especially among party-boat anglers.

SHEEPSHEAD: This popular, fun-to-catch fish ranges from the Atlantic waters off Cape Cod to the Gulf of Mexico. Chunky and deep-bodied, it has with large scales and wide, black, vertical stripes on the body. Its dorsal spines are long

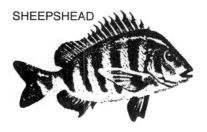

SHEEPSHEAD

and very sharp. "Buck" teeth used for cutting up shellfish and crabs are sheeplike and give this fish its common name. It is found around the pilings of piers and bridges, and around reefs and wrecks. Average weight 1 to 5 pounds; maximum

is over 20 pounds. Still-fishing with fiddler crab bait is the most popular method of fishing for sheepshead. Whole or cut shrimp are also good for bait. Wire leader and good sharp hooks are needed. The mouth, although small, is extremely hard. The sheepshead is a wary fish with a soft bite. Some experience is needed before an angler can set the hook on every nibble. Sheepshead are excellent table fish.

FLOUNDER: Also called flukes, these fish occur in the Atlantic and Gulf of Mexico, and in the Pacific. There are several species, unmistakable because of their extremely com-

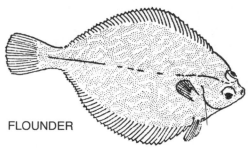

FLOUNDER

pressed bodies, and the characteristic that both eyes are on what appears to be the top of the head, as they lie on the bottom. Flounders usually lie buried in the sand or mud, but they can swim swiftly to capture prey or escape from predators. Coloration depends on the species, but the upper side is usually darker, and is mottled or spotted to camouflage the fish on sandy bottoms; the underside is always white. Species

91

include summer flounder, winter flounder, halibut, California halibut, and others. There are "left-eyed" and "right-eyed" flounder, characterized by which side of the head contains the eyes at adulthood. Young flounders have eyes that appear on each side of the head, like other fishes. But as they mature, one eye migrates left or right, depending on the species. As a rule, flounders weigh from 1 to 20 pounds, with halibuts being largest, especially the Atlantic species, which may weigh up to several hundred pounds. They are fishes of sandy bottoms, in both very shallow and very deep waters. Food consists of all kinds of shellfish and small finfish. They are usually caught by still-fishing in bays, from small boats or jetties and piers, using small hooks and keeping bait on the bottom. Baited hooks should be moved frequently, because flounders are not active swimmers. They prefer to lie buried in the sand and wait for prey to come by, crawling or swimming. Slow drift fishing with live minnows or cut shrimp and slow trolling with small spinners are also effective and attract fish. Flounders are fair fighters, and their flesh is mild delicate, and delicious. They are important commercially.

There are many other saltwater fish that make good catching and fine eating: the huge schools of Silver Hake of the northern Atlantic Coast, the surf-loving whiting, the various rockfish of the Pacific, the California sand and kelp basses, and many others. If you master the exciting art of angling for those listed here, you will be able to catch any of the others you desire. In fact, the chances are that you will probably catch them even when you are not fishing for them!

SHARKS AND SHARK FISHING

ATLANTIC ANGLER'S GUIDE TO SHARKS

The following identification key will help anglers to determine which shark has been caught, from among the many species of sharks found in Atlantic waters:

1. Entire body flattened like a skate: one possibility—ANGEL SHARK

2. Large fleshy projection (barbel) present on each nostril, caudal (tail) fin not separated into two lobes: one possibility—NURSE SHARK

3. Anal fins are not present: two possibilities—SPINY DOGFISH or KITEFIN SHARK

4. Caudal (tail) fin is long as rest of body: two possibilities—
   A. Eye very large—BIGEYE THRESHER
   B. Eyes small—THRESHER SHARK

5. Head is expanded sideways like a shovel or hammer: four possibilities—
   A. Head shovel-shaped—BONNETHEAD SHARK
   B. Head hammer-shaped, anterior margin of head rounded or straight—SMOOTH HAMMERHEAD
   C. Head hammer-shaped, anterior margin of head indented, upper and lower teeth serrated or sawlike, posterior margin of pelvic fins curved—GREAT HAMMERHEAD
   D. Head hammer-shaped, anterior margin of head indented, upper and lower teeth smooth, posterior margin of pelvic fins straight—SCALLOPED HAMMERHEAD

6. Mouth at tip of snout and 6 to 7 prominent ridges occur along the entire length of the back: one possibility—WHALE SHARK

7. A mid-dorsal ridge is present between the first and second dorsal fin: five possibilities—
   A. First and second dorsal fins are about equal in size—SMOOTH DOGFISH
   B. Origin of first dorsal fin over or anterior of free inner angle of pectoral fin—SANDBAR SHARK

93

C. Free tip of second dorsal fin is more than twice as long as height of the fin—SILKY SHARK

D. Fins tipped in white, length of pectoral fin equal to or greater than distance from mouth to last gill opening—WHITETIP SHARK

E. None of the above, upper and lower teeth serrated or sawlike—DUSKY SHARK

8. Ridge on caudal peduncle: five possibilities—

A. Gill openings are as long length of pectoral fins—BASKING SHARK

B. Two ridges or lateral keels present on caudal peduncle—PORBEAGLE SHARK

C. Upper lobe of caudal (tail) fin is at least three times longer than lower lobe—TIGER SHARK

D. None of the above, upper and lower teeth serrated or sawlike—WHITE SHARK

E. None of the above, upper and lower teeth smooth—SHORTFIN MAKO SHARK

9. No mid-dorsal keel or ridges on caudal peduncle, both dorsal fins nearly equal in size: two possibilities—

A. All five gill openings in front of pectoral fins—SAND TIGER SHARK

B. Head very broad and slightly flattened above, distance nostril greater than distances from front of mouth to tip of snout—BULL SHARK

GAME SHARKS

For many years, sharks were considered a menace by all but shark anglers. Many big game anglers now recognize that some sharks are challenging sportfish, and some species are very high-quality food fish. Anglers who have ever tied into a shark of any size will attest that sharks will fight for their lives when hooked, that most sharks are capable of long runs, and that they are capable of great leaps, spins, powerful head shaking—even some tailwalking. Experienced shark anglers compare the tenacity of sharks with fighting fish such as tuna, sailfish, swordfish, and tarpon. In fact, the IGFA has included seven sharks on their gamefish list: the blue shark, mako shark, hammerhead, porbeagle, thresher, tiger and great white shark. All of these are available to the angler that fishes the South Atlantic Ocean or the Gulf of Mexico, and some of these are found in the Pacific Ocean.

Shark fishing is like fishing for any other gamefish; to pursue with success any branch of fishing, the senses and habits of fishes to be fished should be carefully studied. Sharks are opportunistic feeders, much less selective in their choice of food than most bony fishes.

SHARK IDENTIFICATION

It is important for shark anglers to learn the superficial structure and characteristics of sharks. Unlike bony fishes, sharks come in three colors: shades of brown, gray and blue. As is true for bony fishes, positive identification of sharks begins with body outline. Many marine biologists, serious scuba divers, and experienced shark anglers are able to identify sharks by silhouette drawings. Sharks have no true bones in their skeletons; they consist entirely of cartilage, as do the skeletons of rays and skates, to which sharks are closely related.

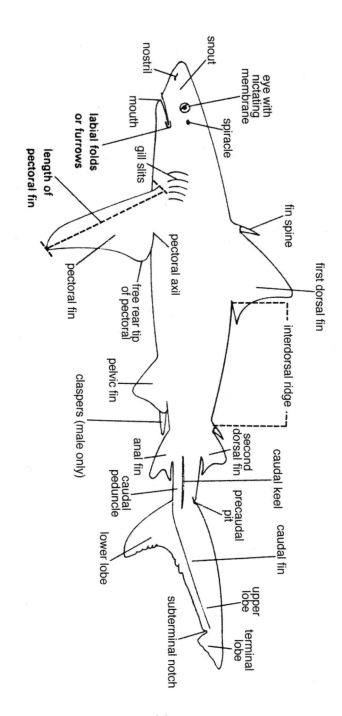

snout

nostril

eye with
nictating
membrane

mouth

**labial folds
or furrows**

spiracle

gill slits

**length of
pectoral fin**

pectoral axil

pectoral fin

free rear tip
of pectoral

pelvic fin

claspers (male only)

anal fin

caudal
peduncle

fin spine

first dorsal fin

interdorsal ridge

second
dorsal fin

caudal keel

precaudal
pit

caudal fin

lower lobe

subterminal notch

upper
lobe

terminal
lobe

96

GREAT WHITE

PORBEAGLE

HAMMERHEAD

THRESHER

MAKO

BLUE

TIGER

SOURCE:
INTERNATIONAL
GAME FISH
ASSOCIATION

IGFA GAME SHARKS

FISHING TIPS

Have you ever stopped to wonder why some fishermen always seem to come back with fish? Is it luck? Not exactly. Consistent success results from having the right equipment and keeping it in good condition, knowing when and where to fish, what bait or lures to use, and developing excellent technique in hooking and landing a fish.

Reels are indispensable casting machines that should be oiled, adjusted, and running as smooth as a fine watch before they are put into use. Too many fishermen ignore their reels until they malfunction. This could happen during a fight with the biggest fish of your life! How about the rod? Guides should be checked for breaks, rough spots and the windings. Ferrules should be tight, the shaft free of fractures. The line? Check the first six feet for nicks, abrasions and brittleness. Should you find any of these, discard the length of the trouble plus an extra foot for insurance. The leader, whether monofilament or wire, should get the same sort of inspection. If you use sunscreen or suntan lotion or oil, wash your hands well. If no soap is available, use sand and saltwater. These substances will tend to rot your fishing line and can also render your live or artificial baits useless. Everything ready? Make certain the hooks you use are extremely sharp when you buy them, then keep them that way. Next, check that you have control of your tackle. Spare rods should be secure in proper holders, the tackle box should be closed and secured, loose lures should be hung where someone won't sit on them, and enough space should be allowed between casters so they won't hook each other.

A sharp hook is needed because in many cases it is the fish, not the fisherman, that sets the hook during the initial strike. Many fishermen use limber rods that make it difficult, if not impossible, to set the hook hard when a fish hits. A light line and drag accentuate the problem: you must have the drag fairly light to keep from breaking the line, and yet when the drag is adjusted in this manner it is hard to really to set the hook on the strike.

SALTWATER FISH
PREFERRED TEMPERATURE CHART
All readings are in Fahrenheit

Albacore Tuna	59 Degrees	Striped Bass	60 Degrees
Pompano	77 Degrees	Bluefish	68 Degrees
Amberjack	60 Degrees	Yellowtail (Calif.)	65 Degrees
Red Drum (redfish)	71 Degrees	Blue Marlin	78 Degrees
Atlantic Cod	44–49+ Degrees	Swordfish	58 Degrees
Red Snapper	57 Degrees	Bonefish	75 Degrees
Atlantic Bonito	64 Degrees	Tarpon	76 Degrees
Sailfish	79 Degrees	Dolphin	75 Degrees
Mackerel	46 Degrees	Tautog	70 Degrees
Sand Seatrout	95 Degrees	King Mackerel	65 Degrees
Barracuda	75 Degrees	Wahoo	70–86 Degrees
Snook	70–75 Degrees	Permit	72 Degrees
Black Marlin	75–70 Degrees	White Marlin	70-80 Degrees
Spotted Seatrout	72 Degrees	Pollock	50 Degrees
Bluefin Tuna	68 Degrees	Winter Flounder	48–52 Degrees

Fish have lower and upper temperature tolerances that are usually about 10 degrees apart. For instance, the striped bass prefers a water temperature of about 60°F, avoiding water colder than 54°F or warmer than 77°F.

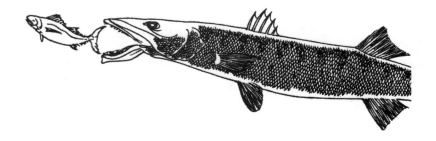

Fishing Knots

The knot you tie can mean the difference between losing or landing a fish. The knots on the following pages have been proven effective in use. If properly formed using a quality product line, they should test close to or equal to the breaking load of the line.

A few basic rules can assure that knots will deliver their full potential in holding power: (1) Where turns are required around the standing line, keep them separated, then pull them together in a neat spiral when tightening the knot; (2) Such knots hold best in low pound-class lines. Increased line diameters make it difficult to pull coils tight. Don't expect full-rated strength from knots like the Improved Clinch in lines over the 20-lb (10 kg) class; (3) When double lines are used, as in the Palomar or Spider Hitch, keep them as parallel as possible. Avoid twisting the knot as it is being tied; (4) Always pull knots up as tightly as possible, using even, steady pressure. Knot slippage under pressure can cut the line.

Knots to hold terminal tackle

These are vital connections between your line and the terminal tackle. The following knots have proven to be dependable:

IMPROVED CLINCH KNOT
An old standby.

1. Pass line through eye of hook, swivel or lure. Double back and make five turns around the standing line. Hold coils in place; thread end of line through first loop above the eye, then through big loop, as shown.

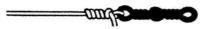

2. Hold tag end and standing line while coils are pulled up. Take care that coils are in spiral, not overlapping each other. Slide tight against eye. Clip tag end.

The fishing knots on these pages are reprinted courtesy of the DuPont Company, Wilmington, Delaware from "Fishing Knots You Can Depend On..."

PALOMAR KNOT
Easier to tie right, and consistently the strongest knot known to hold terminal tackle.

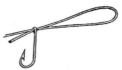

1. Double about 4" of line and pass loop through eye.

2. Let book hang loose and tie overhand knot in doubled line. Avoid twisting the lines and don't tighten knot.

3. Pull loop of line far enough to pass it over hook, swivel or lure. Make sure loop passes completely over this attachment.
4. Pull both tag end and standing line to tighten. Clip about ⅛" from knot.

SPIDER HITCH

This is a faster, easier knot to form a double line. Under steady pressure it is equally strong but does not have the resilience of the Bimini Twist under sharp impact. Not practical with lines above the 30-lb (15 kg) class.

1. Form a loop of the leader length desired. Near the point where it meets the standing line, twist a section into a small reverse loop.

2. Hold small loop between thumb and forefinger, with thumb extended well above finger and loop standing out beyond end of thumb.

3. Wind double line around both thumb and loop, taking five turns. Pass remainder of large loop through the smaller one and pull to make five turns. Unwind off the thumb.

4. Pull turns around the base of the loop up tight and snip off tag end.

Attaching swivel or snap to double line

OFFSHORE SWIVEL KNOT

1. Slip loop end of double line through eye of swivel. Rotate loop end a half-rum to put a single twist between loop and swivel eye.

2. Pass the loop with the twist over the swivel. Hold end of the loop, plus both legs of the double line, with one hand. Let swivel slide to the other end of the double loops now formed.

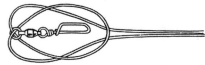

3. Still holding loop and lines with one hand, use other to rotate swivel through center of both loops, at least six times.

4. Continue holding both legs of double line tightly, but release end of loop. Pull on swivel and loops of line will begin to gather.

5. To draw knot tight, grip swivel with pliers and push loops toward eye with fingers, while still keeping standing lines of the double line pulled tight.

The Uni-Knot System

One basic knot can be varied to meet virtually every knot-tying need, in either fresh- or saltwater fishing. That was the guiding principle used by Vic Dunaway, author of numerous books on fishing, in developing the Uni-Knot system:

A. TYING TO TERMINAL TACKLE

1. Run line through eye of hook, swivel or lure at least 6" and fold to make two parallel lines. Bring end of line back in a circle toward hook or lure.

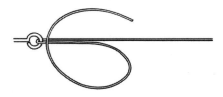

101

2. Make six turns with tag end around the double line and through the circle. Hold double line at point where it passes through eye and pull tag end to snug up turns.

3. Now pull standing line to slide knot up against eye.

4. Continue pulling until knot is tight. Trim tag end flush with closest coil of knot. Uni-Knot will not slip.

B. LOOP CONNECTION

Tie same knot as above to point where turns are snugged up around standing line. Slide knot toward eye until loop size desired is reached. Pull tag end with pliers to maximum tightness. This gives lure a natural free movement in water. When fish is hooked, knot will slide tight against eye.

C. JOINING LINES

1. Overlap ends of two lines of about same diameter for about 6". With one end, form Uni-Knot circle, crossing the two lines about midway of overlapped distance.

2. Tie basic Uni-Knot, making six turns around the two lines.

Loop knots

The Surgeon's End Loop and the Dropper Loop can be used to connect leaders or other terminal tackle quickly.

SURGEON'S END LOOP

1. Double end of line to form loop and tie overhand knot at base of double line.
2. Leave loop open in knot and bring doubled line through once more.

3. Hold standing line and tag end and pull loop to tighten knot. Size of loop can be controlled by pulling loose knot to desired point and holding it while knot is tightened. Clip tag end.

DROPPER LOOP

To form a loop which stands out from line above a sinker or other terminal rig:

1. Form a loop in the line.
2. Pull one side of the loop down and begin taking turns with it around the standing line. Keep point where turns are made open so turns gather equally on each side.

3. After eight to ten turns, reach through center opening and pull remaining loop through. Keep finger in this loop so it will not spring back.

4. Hold loop with teeth and pull both ends of line, making turns gather on either side of loop.

5. Set knot by pulling lines as tightly as possible. Tightening coils will make loop stand out perpendicular to line.

Knots to form double lines
Used primarily for offshore trolling, a double line creates a long loop of line which is stronger than the single strand of the standing line.

BIMINI TWIST
These directions may be used to tie double lines of five feet or less. For longer double-line sections, two people may be required, to hold the line and make initial twists.

1. Measure a little more than twice the footage you'll want for the double line. Bring end back to standing line and hold together. Rotate end of loop 20 times, putting twists in it.

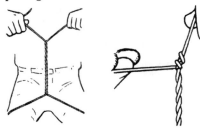

2. Spread loop to force twists together about 10" below tag end. Step both feet through loop and bring it up around knees so pressure can be placed on column of twists by spreading knees apart.

3. With twists forced tightly together, hold standing line in one hand with tension just slightly off the vertical position. With other hand, move tag end to position at right angle to twists. Keeping tension on loop with knees, gradually ease tension of tag end so it will roll over the column of twists, beginning just below the upper twist.

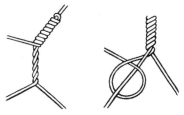

4. Spread legs apart slowly to maintain pressure on loop. Steer tag end into a tight spiral coil as it continues to roll over twisted line.

5. When spiral of tag end has rolled over column of twists, continue keeping knee pressure on loop and move hand which has held standing line down to grasp knot. Place finger in crotch of line where loop joins knot to prevent slippage of last turn. Take half-hitch with tag end around nearest leg of loop and pull up tight.

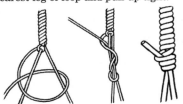

6. With half-hitch holding knot, release knee pressure but keep loop stretched out tight. Using remaining tag end, take half-hitch around both legs of loop, but do not pull tight.

7. Make two more turns with the tag end around both legs of the loop, winding inside the bend of line formed by the loose half-hitch and toward the main knot. Pull tag end slowly, forcing the three loops to gather in a spiral.

8. When loops are pulled up neatly against main knot, tighten to lock knot in place. Trim tag end about ¼" from knot.

103

JANSIK SPECIAL

A knot of proven strength.

1. Run about five inches of line through eye of hook on lure; bring it around in a circle and run it through again.

2. Make a second circle, parallel with the first, and pass end of line through eye a third time.

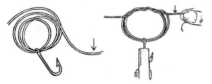

3. Bend standing part of line around the two circles. Bring tag end around in a third circle and wrap it three times around the three parallel lines.

4. Hold hook, swivel or lure with pliers. Hold standing line with other hand and tag end in teeth. Pull all three to tighten. (Arrows identify standing line.)

SNELLING A HOOK

Using this common snell, hook and leader combinations can be made to suit the length and strength needed for various types of fishing.

1. Insert one end of leader material through eye of hook just past turn and barb. Pass other end through eye in opposite direction, leaving large loop hanging down.

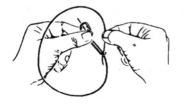

2. Hold both lines along shank. Use line hanging from eye to wind tight coils around shank and both lines, from eye toward hook. Take 5 to 10 turns.

3. Move fingers to hold coils tightly in place. Pull leader extending from eye until entire loop has passed under coils.

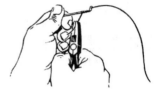

4. With coils snugged up neatly, use pliers to pull tag end, cinching up snell. Clip off tag end.

Knots to tie line-to-line and line-to-leader

These two knots are most often used to join line. Tie the blood knot for two lines of about the same diameter, the surgeon's knot to join a leader to line where the diameters vary considerably.

BLOOD KNOT

1. Lay ends of lines alongside each other, overlapping about 6" of line. Hold lines at midpoint. Take five turns around standing line with tag end and bring end back between the two strands, where they are being held.

CARING FOR YOUR FISH

The fish you catch should be kept alive in the water from which they have been removed, either by placing them on a stringer or in a floating live bag. Some boats are equipped with a live box which protects fish from the direct rays of the sun. Light, inexpensive Styrofoam boxes with ice are also very good for keeping your fish fresh.

If you have to keep your fish for a few days before getting them home to the freezer, you should clean them at the end of each fishing day. Once cleaned, they should be wrapped in plastic and packed in ice or frozen with dry ice. When using natural ice make sure that the thaw-water does not make direct contact with the fish, or it will soak the flesh soft and render it tasteless.

When preparing fish for the freezer, place whole, gutted, scaled or scaleless, headless fish in a half-gallon milk carton, then fill it to the top with water and place it in the freezer, uncovered. When ready to cook the fish, thaw it completely, then scale and fillet it. Do not freeze fish fillets in this manner, as much of the flavor will be lost during thawing. Fillets should be wrapped in plastic and then wrapped again in freezer paper. Always date your packages. Fish can be kept frozen for a period of three months with no changes to the quality.

FILLETING FISH

The enjoyment that comes from eating fresh fish is greatly enhanced if you don't have to spend a lot of time picking out bones, especially if you are feeding small children who cannot do the job themselves.

The flavor of most fish is much improved by filleting. Use a sharp fillet knife and follow the steps below, and you should have no problem:

1. Lay the fish on a cutting board. Make the first cut behind the gill, at a diagonal, cutting toward the head. Stop at the backbone.

2. Turn the blade of the knife flat against the backbone and cut the length and width of the body, through the rib cage,

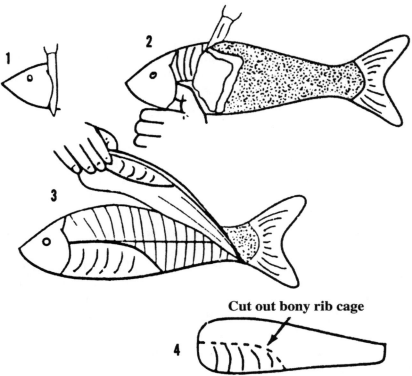

Cut out bony rib cage

and then follow the backbone to the tail fin. Do not cut through the skin at the base of the tail. Leave it intact and lift the fillet meat off the backbone.

3. Flip the fillet as if you were opening a hinged lid, laying it back against the cutting board (still attached by the piece of skin at the tail). Skin the fillet by running the knife between the meat and skin. Then turn the fish over and repeat the procedure for the second fillet.

4. The final step is to cut the rib cage out of the fillet meat. The result will be two boneless fillets.

KEEPING YOUR HOOKS SHARP

Make sure that hooks are sharp when you buy them and then keep them that way.

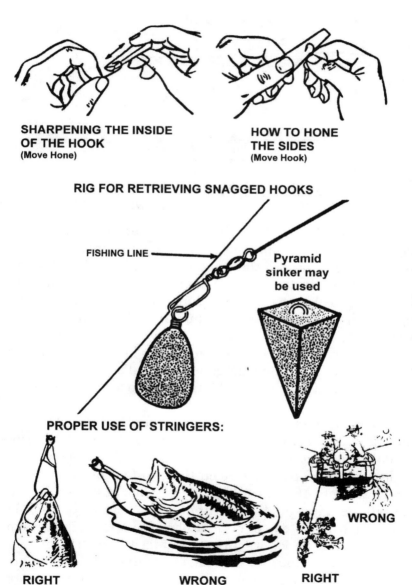

SHARPENING THE INSIDE OF THE HOOK
(Move Hone)

HOW TO HONE THE SIDES
(Move Hook)

RIG FOR RETRIEVING SNAGGED HOOKS

FISHING LINE

Pyramid sinker may be used

PROPER USE OF STRINGERS:

RIGHT

WRONG

WRONG

RIGHT

FIRST AID FOR THE ANGLER

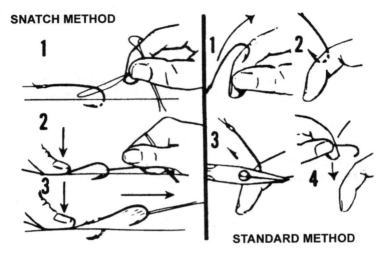

SNATCH METHOD

STANDARD METHOD

REMOVING FISHHOOKS: Before removing a hook by any method, apply antiseptic to the hook-imbedded area. Remove the hook by the snatch method or the standard method as illustrated above. After the hook is removed, allow the wound to bleed freely for a couple of minutes before cleaning it with antiseptic and applying an antibiotic salve. Cover it with a bandage. Should the hook be deeply imbedded into the flesh, near or in the eye, temple, or spine, seek medical help immediately at an emergency medical center or hospital. In such a situation, do not attempt to remove the hook by any method.

Necessary items for an emergency first-aid kit: (1) Gauze pads (2" x 2"), (2) Roll of one-inch adhesive tape, (3) Adhesive bandages (a variety of sizes), (4) Unopened single-edged razor blades, (5) Small pair of wire cutters, (6) Pair of tweezers, (7) Aspirin tablets, (8) Salt tablets, (9) Alcohol (2-oz. plastic bottle), (10) Betadine or other antiseptic (2-oz. plastic bottle), (11) Tube of antibiotic salve, (12) Alcohol sponges, (13) Pre-sunburn lotion, (14) Adolph's unseasoned meat tenderizer.

Be sure that your tetanus shots are up-to-date. This precautionary measure alone will prevent many unnecessary infections related to fishing accidents.

FIRST AID TREATMENTS

FISH HOOK REMOVAL

Apply antiseptic before removing the hook. After the hook is removed allow the wound to bleed freely for a couple of minutes before washing it with Betadine and applying the anti-biotic salve. Cover with Band Aid. If the hook is imbedded deep into the flesh or is close to — or in the eye, temple or spine, see a doctor immediately.

CATFISH SPINES

Do not take injuries by catfish spines lightly! Let the wound bleed freely, then clean it with antiseptic, apply an antibiotic salve and cover with a bandage.

STINGRAY WOUND

Place stricken area in hottest water possible. Keep immersed for 30 minutes to an hour. Pain will be relieved. If wound is large, a physician may be required to close it. When fishing in the surf, boat shoes should be worn, but even then you should shuffle your feet to scare off the stingrays that may be buried in the sand.

SEA URCHIN SPINES

All spines should be removed carefully. If area appears red, or if painful swelling around the wound occurs, surgery may be required to remove broken spines that remain in the flesh. Sea urchin spines are another powerful argument for wearing boat shoes when in the surf.

FISH BITES

Most fish bites can be treated in the same manner as a catfish sting. However, if the bite is severe (say, from a shark or barracuda), apply a tourniquet or direct pressure to stop the bleeding and consult a doctor immediately.

JELLYFISH AND SEA ANEMONE STINGS

Symptoms are blisters, rash, and vomiting accompanied by pain in the affected area. Remove tentacles with cloth or paper. Mix a paste of alcohol and unseasoned Adolph's meat tenderizer. Cover the stings with paste and with a bandage. If the stings cover a wide area and the pain is severe, see a doctor as soon as possible. To prevent such stings, stay clear of all jellyfish.

OVERHEATING

Move to a cool, shaded area and take one or two salt tablets every two or three hours. Drink adequate fluids. If symptoms persist beyond mild stomach cramps, with dizziness or shock symptoms, seek a doctor's care immediately.

SUNBURN

Fishermen should always wear sunscreen, sufficient clothing and a head covering. If burned, but not blistered, apply cold milk compresses every 30 minutes for several hours, then treat with a mild moisturizing lotion like Noxema. Polarizing sunglasses that provide UV protection are essential to prevent eye damage from the sun.

GLOVES

Always keep a good pair of work gloves handy to avoid line burn, and to prevent cuts and scratches when removing your catch from the hook. They also protect from the poisonous spines of catfish and the spines and teeth from other fishes, particularly barracuda and bluefish.

ESTIMATING A DEAD FISH'S WEIGHT
USING A TAPE MEASURE
(Sharks and bony fishes)

The International Game Fish Association has devised a mathematical formula that enables an angler to obtain the approximate weight of sharks and other deep-bodied fishes. The formula is:

$$\frac{\text{Girth in inches}^2 \text{ x Length in inches}}{800} = \text{Weight in pounds}$$

The girth, or measurement around the fish, is squared (multiplied by itself). This figure is then multiplied by the fish's length in inches, and the final result is divided by 800.

Example: If a fish's circumference at its thickest part is 30 inches, and the length from the tip of its snout to the fork of its tail is 46 inches, we may apply the formula as follows:

$$\frac{30 \text{ x } 30 \text{ x } 46}{800} = \frac{41,400}{800} = 51.75 \text{ pounds}$$

The next time you catch a large fish and are able to weigh it, try the formula, and then compare it to the actual weight. You will be surprised at how well this works.

OCEAN TEMPERATURE

Temperature plays a very important part in the production and well-being of all organisms, both on land and in water. The growth rate of all organisms and the breakdown of dead organics are more rapid in warmer water. When enough nutrients are present, the productivity of the sea can be extremely high.

Temperature in the open ocean varies from about 28.4 degrees F. to 86°F. Some areas, like the Persian Gulf, exceed 90°F; during summer months in shallow inshore waters, temperatures as high as 96.8°F. have been recorded. Ocean water is much more uniform in temperature; 75% is in the range of 32°F. to 42.8°F. and 33% is between 33.8°F. to 42.8°F.

Day-to-day changes in the temperature of seawater depend upon cloud conditions, but the daily variation is rarely more than 1 degree F., and this change takes place only in a thin surface layer. On a clear day temperatures may, at times, rise as much as 4 degrees F. The daily change in water temperature is small compared to air or land temperature because about five times as much heat is necessary to produce the same temperature change in water as in air.

In cold seas, water temperature is about equal from the surface to the bottom all year round. In temperate areas, a fairly thin layer of the upper surface (only some tens of meters in some places) is warmed up during the summer. In subtropical and tropical areas, the surface layers become much warmer than the deep and may penetrate down to 600 to 1,500 feet.

The deep and bottom layers of the open oceans are always cold and most of the water comes originally from the Arctic or Antarctic seas. Animal life in these cold-water layers consists of cold-resistant forms, and is generally very sparse.